A White House in Gascony

A White House in Gascony

Escape to the Old French South

REX GRIZELL

LONDON
VICTOR GOLLANCZ LTD
1992

The people and places described in this book are
all real but out of consideration and perhaps fear
of the consequences the names in most cases have
been changed.

First published in Great Britain 1992
by Victor Gollancz Ltd
14 Henrietta Street, London WC2E 8QJ

© Rex Grizell 1992

A catalogue record for this book is
available from the British Library

ISBN 0 575 05400 X √

Illustrations by Gillian Hunt

Typeset at CentraCet, Linton, Cambridge
and printed in Great Britain by
St Edmundsbury Press Ltd, Bury St Edmunds, Suffolk

CONTENTS

Author's Note

Gascony is not today a precise term. Like other famous regions of France, Périgord and the Dauphine, for example, it has a real but no longer an official existence. This old province of south-west France was originally a Duchy. By inheritance it became part of the greater Duchy of Aquitaine, which for three hundred years was English. Today Gascony, which has no defined limits, lies at the heart of the modern administrative region of Aquitaine and consists of the department of Gers with important areas of the adjacent departments. The people born and bred within the old province still think of themselves as Gascons, are proud of it and keep alive the language and traditions of their past.

Gascony is to the western part of southern France, what inland Provence is to the east. Its capital, the old city of Auch, is further south than Avignon, and there is no nerve-wracking Mistral to spoil the warm and sunny climate. Despite its lovely and varied scenery and its long association with England, it is, for some inexplicable reason, less well-known than Provence.

Chapter One

IS THAT ALL? JUST A CAT?

Some people have all the luck. The trouble is it's almost always other people. There was a chap called Hessel Vogelfang who went for a holiday stroll in the Austrian Alps. He was appropriately dressed in leather shorts with leather braces, big boots, and a hat with a feather. Nevertheless, he slipped and fell over a 500-foot precipice. Certain death, you might think. But not for Mr Vogelfang, who, despite his name, was lucky. His stout leather braces caught on the branch of a tree about twenty feet below the edge, and there he hung for two days and two nights, until a rescue party hauled him up, still wearing his hat. When asked how he felt, he replied that he was perfectly all right, but very hungry.

I cannot say that a similar thing happened to us, although a precipice was there on our right, and we, too, were suddenly given the old one-two by Lady Luck, bad then good. We were returning from a motoring holiday in Spain and were crossing the Pyrenees from Pamplona to St Jean-Pied-de-Port, so that we could see Roncesvalles, where the legendary hero Roland, one of Charlemagne's generals, met his death. In the narrow pass his army was cut to pieces by a superior force of Gascons. We found it a disappointing place, grim, grey, misty, cold, and dripping with damp. We hardly paused, before beginning the long descent into France. The road had a stone parapet on the right and a precipitous drop beyond it; on the left was the mountain, rising in a stone cliff.

The bad luck was that, about a third of the way down, I put my foot on the brake to slow down for a sharp bend, and nothing happened. The pedal went straight to the floor with no effect. I changed down a gear but it was too late. The car hit the parapet in the bend and was thrown straight across the road, where it hit the cliff, bounced off, spun round and stopped. The good luck was that there was nothing else about, and we had stopped on the right side of the road. The further bad luck was that we were miles from anywhere and the car was undrivable, both front wheels buckled and the coachwork a write-off. The further good luck was that neither my wife, Marie-Anne, who was in the passenger seat, nor I suffered anything more than a nasty shake-up. We stood by the wreck and waited. Eventually a car came down, blew its horn at us, as if we were obstructing the road on purpose, and drove on. A few minutes later another driver came by, took in the situation and stopped. Marie-Anne stayed with the car, while the driver gave me a lift to the gendarmerie in the nearest village, where I reported the accident and got things moving.

So, in a way we were as lucky as Herr Vogelfang, and not so hungry. Lucky, because it was this accident which led us, indirectly, to live where we live now, in one of the loveliest and least-known corners of France, the former province of Gascony.

We had been thinking for some time of buying a house in France, and perhaps moving there permanently, but we had been undecided as to where to go. We wanted the warm south, but had ruled out Provence. The coastal strip, delightful forty years ago, is now hopelessly overcrowded and far too expensive, and inland, though spectacular, the country was infertile, poverty-stricken, with a harsh climate and embittered people. We had intended to spend the last week of our holiday driving along the French side of the Pyrenees to Perpignan and then east towards Montpellier and Nîmes, exploring Languedoc and getting an idea of property prices.

Instead, since there were formalities to be dealt with as a result of the accident, and as we felt the need for a couple of days' rest after the shock, we stayed in this south-west corner of France. We hired the cheapest viable car we could find and idled slowly and erratically northwards, exploring the region. We looked at Bayonne, and Biarritz, which had been good enough for the Emperor Louis Napoleon and Queen Victoria, we went inland to Mont-de-Marsan and Auch, and tasted our first Armagnac brandy in wayside farms in the lovely, still unchanged countryside of the

Gers department, which bred the Three Musketeers. We zigzagged to look at the great bay and vast sandy beaches of Arcachon, admired the stylish centre of Bordeaux, and moved inland again to see the picturesque bastide villages like Fources, Larresingle, Monpazier and Monflanquin. Everywhere we ate splendid, copious meals at ridiculously cheap prices in charming old inns. Towards the end of the week we travelled north to Bergerac and the Dordogne, and on back to London.

We had been impressed by the beauty and variety of the countryside, and not least by the property prices. A small château in reasonable order and with a few acres could be bought for the price of a one-bedroomed flat on the Côte d'Azur. Also, we had been assured that it was usually mild in winter and the hottest part of France in summer – it is on the same latitude as the Italian Riviera. We decided that halfway between the Dordogne and the Pyrenees and halfway between the Bordeaux vineyards and those around Cahors, somewhere in the former province of Gascony, would be about right.

In late summer we returned to look at houses and were soon enjoying the first samples of the off-beat nature of the Gascons and their 'pays'. Many others were to follow. We began in the north of the region and worked south. We liked the second house that we saw but, being thorough, we visited a number of agents in different towns. They were a strange group. One of them kept a shoe shop, one sold houses from his home address, which still had a sign reading 'Electricien' at the gate – he was making the transition, he said, but if we should ever want any rewiring done, could we bear him in mind? – and one of them had a facial tic, so that he winked frequently, giving half of what he said a 'double entendre'. It was difficult to deal with a man who said things like 'Of course the roof does not leak' and followed it with a crafty wink. Between them they showed us a lot of pleasant properties at reasonable prices. We also saw a number of what can best be described as stone elephants, which the agents, knowing I was English and therefore mad, offered us hoping we would be daft enough to buy.

Some of these were odd places with even odder inhabitants. There was the house which the owner said was built from the stones of a ruined medieval castle and on its foundations. To prove it he took us down a dark spiral stone staircase to a large underground room with bare stone walls.

'Now look at this,' he said. 'Walls six feet thick, you can't hear a thing through them. I come down here sometimes to play the trumpet. Perfect for a discotheque. Of course, it was originally a dungeon.' He paused. 'Still a good place to torture people.' We had no victims in mind, and we did not stay long.

One extraordinary house stood alone on a plateau, about a mile from any other habitation. It may once have been a farmhouse but it had been converted beyond all recognition. 'No expense spared,' said the agent, and it was probably the only time I have believed this statement. It was stone built and it looked inside and out as if each stone had been individually scrubbed. It had every gadget known to man; its kitchen would have frightened the cookery editor of *Good Housekeeping*. The bathroom had a jacuzzi as well as an ordinary bath and an enclosed shower in which the water came at you from all sides as well as from overhead. The couple who were living there were equally unusual, a blonde not much less restored than the house, and a dark, lean, youngish man who looked like Sean Connery in a filthy temper. Having shaken hands they left us with the agent and went out, she in red leather from head to foot, he in a long black leather coat and a white snap-brim hat. The agent showed us the house, including a bedroom where a double wardrobe had been left open. 'Ah,' said the agent, and went across to close it, but not before we had seen that it contained nothing but shelves of women's shoes and boots, all in different colours, many of them shiny, and all with four-inch stiletto heels.

Perhaps it was no coincidence that it was the agent with the shoe shop who had this house on his list. It must really have cost a fortune to restore, and was worth about double the asking price. I said as much.

'Marseille, milieu,' said the agent mysteriously. 'Vous savez, l'argent,' he shrugged.

I looked at Marie-Anne. 'He means he's a gangster in the Marseille underworld. Money no object,' she said.

'What's he doing here then?'

'Hideaway,' muttered the agent, as if he understood my question. 'He's got houses all over the place. Blocks of flats, as well.'

We were tempted, but it really was too far from anywhere. And there was always a chance that he'd put a foot wrong one day, and some of his ex-friends might call, breathing blood and vengeance, unaware that he had moved.

Then there was a property described to us as a 'castel', a comfortable little château. It had a magnificent oak staircase, wide and shallow enough to drive a tractor up, and the main bedroom was approximately the size of a tennis court, and we noticed a number of screens that clearly had more to do with draughts than modesty. We recalled that the agent had described the accommodation as 'roomy' which I had taken to mean the same as it does to English estate agents – impossible to heat. Sure enough the owners, a retired French admiral and his wife, were living in a corner of the ground floor in two rooms next to the kitchen.

We found that quite a lot of the terms used by the French estate agents had the same meaning as those used by their British counterparts. 'Interesting' meant architecturally indescribable, and 'much sought after' seemed to equal impossible to find. With a good deal of patience we did eventually find such a place. It was owned by a sculptor, described by the agent as 'Danish, I think, or something like that, and a bit eccentric', but who seemed to us rather a long way round the bend. He began by asking us to take our shoes off before we came in, and appeared to think we had come to look at his work rather than as possible house buyers. He showed us many pieces, explaining the finer points of his technique – hardly necessary, since he had only one theme. Every single piece was a phallic symbol. There was even something like a model of a Viking longboat with a phallic prow, and what seemed at first glance to be one of those elongated versions of the Virgin Mary was on closer inspection something quite different. As we expressed no more than a polite interest in his work, he eventually showed us the house which, he said, had been on the pilgrims' route to St James of Compostela, and had a medieval bread oven as well as a small chapel. Judging by the odour of medieval drains which permeated the whole building, nothing had been done to the plumbing since the last pilgrim left. We didn't stay long there, either.

Having failed to unload any of the weird stuff, the agents became more formal and more boring in their suggestions, and eventually we returned to the second house we had seen and arranged to buy it.

So it was chance that brought us to this house in an orchard on the northern edge of the old province of Gascony. Without that accident we might not even have visited this region, but, hardly more than six months after we started looking, there we were, Marie-Anne and I, sitting together side by side at the bottom of the stairs in our new home. There was nowhere else to sit. There was absolutely nothing in the old house but spiders, not all dead, and the dust and fluff left after furniture which had not been cleaned under for years, perhaps generations, had been taken away, and the marks where unknown pictures had hung. Monsieur Rambaud, the extraordinary man from whom we had bought the house, had left almost nothing, not even the old stone baskets of grapes and peaches from either side of the porch, which Marie-Anne had liked so much, and which with such gallantry he had promised to leave her.

So there we were eight hundred miles south of lately abandoned Westminster, emigrants to the warm south of France, where we planned to live happily in peace and relative comfort. In the mean time we sat at the bottom of the stairs, waiting for our furniture to arrive from England. Ten o'clock on the morning of 28th March, without fail, Mr Davies had said, or was it Mr Turner? We could see straight down the tiled hall, through the glazed front door, down the cedar-lined drive to where the pantechnicon containing everything we possessed in the world, except this empty house and the ancient sports saloon in which we had arrived with our black cat, Cleo, would turn in. Any minute now. Only it didn't.

We talked, eagerly at first, about our plans, then walked around a bit trying to decide what we could do with each room. Now that all the splendid antique furniture had gone, the decor seemed tatty. The floors creaked.

'That looks like a damp patch,' I said.

The square at Monpazier, one of the region's walled villages.

'It is a damp patch. There's another in that corner.'

We sat down again, and began to reassure each other. That, after all, was what we had come for, to restore an old house. After two hundred years it was bound to be a bit rough around the edges, but essentially it was a lovely place. It was, wasn't it? I mean, you could see that at a glance.

'We should have looked closer,' said Marie-Anne.

'It will seem different once the furniture is in.'

'Where is it then?'

Good question. It was now well after eleven. 'You can't expect them to do a move of that distance and arrive on the dot.'

'I suppose not. No, of course not.'

All the same I began to feel the first faint twinge of anxiety. This was no 'résidence secondaire'. This was it. There was no comfortable house or flat waiting for us back in London, if things didn't work out. After thirty years of married life, of bringing up the children, of pleasant suburban houses, and finally, a rather nice town house in Pimlico, we had burnt our boats. Sold up. Gone away. Retired to the deep south of France. Why, for God's sake? I must have been mad. I looked sideways at my wife. What on earth had made her agree? True, she was French, but that could only be a small part of the answer for she had lived more than twice as long in England as in France, which from the age of four to seventeen she had known only from the inside of a convent anyway, and since then had seen it only during holidays with the children. So, why? I didn't know. Neither did she. She told me so often during the next few years.

Time went by. We became less excited and more worried. Conversation did one of the few things it can do. It flagged.

'I wish they'd come,' she said, sadly.

'If they don't, we'll just have to go back to the hotel for a night and sort things out tomorrow.'

'What about Cleo?'

Our city cat, black as night and mysterious as an Egyptian goddess, had already disappeared. The transition from the back-yards and basement courts of Westminster to the limitless country-side had been too much for a cat that had started life in Battersea Dogs' Home and had never seen a blade of grass before. She had been given to our daughter, Ariane, as a fifteenth birthday present by one of her schoolfriends. She had staggered out of her basket, so small and weak that she could hardly stand, but well able to pee on the carpet. She had soon learned better manners, and how to drape herself on soft cushions, preferably white, and how to swing on net curtains.

She had left the sybaritic life with regret, not taking at all kindly to the car journey in a basket all the way to Portsmouth, nor to being left all night in the car on the ferry to Le Havre, where she had made her own significant entrance.

'Le Havre,' I said to Marie-Anne. She smiled, forgetting for the moment the missing furniture van.

We had arrived at Le Havre about seven o'clock on a cold Sunday morning in March. It was a day on which very few other people, apart from some lorry drivers, had chosen to cross the Channel. We had nothing with us but our overnight bag, and nothing to declare but Cleo. As we had painstakingly filled in a flurry of forms from the Ministry of Health relating to the export of cats, which we were supposed to present to the Customs authorities, we went to the Douanes.

There was no one there. Anyone who wants to smuggle a ton of drugs into France could do worse than choose first thing on a wet Sunday morning in March. I am sure we could have driven off unchallenged. But we had the forms, so we waited. Presently a pink-faced, gangly youth, who seemed about seventeen, pulling on the jacket of a Customs uniform much too large for him, and with his tie viciously knotted outside his shirt collar, stumbled into the office, sat down gingerly at the desk, dithered among the papers, looked up, looked down, and was clearly very ill at ease. We offered Cleo's 'papers'. He took them as if they might have been contaminated with the plague, looked at the front, looked at the back, turned them over again, and stared into space. He had clearly never seen such a document before.

At length he swallowed. 'Is that all? Just a cat?'

For good measure we gave him our copy of the bulky documents listing everything we were bringing into France, but which we knew would be cleared at Périgueux by the removals company.

'There's these, if you want to see them,' said my wife in French. A wave of panic crossed his face. He looked around as if for help.

Two of the lorry drivers, sensing a situation, and looking as if they could deal with anything that might arise, ambled across.

'Bonjour, m'sieur, dame,' they said to us. 'Hey, Albert, bonjour. Everything all right?'

'Bonjour, monsieur Charles,' said Albert, full of respect. 'I'm not sure . . . it's this cat . . . and then there's all this . . .'

'What's the problem?' the lorry driver asked Marie-Anne.

She explained that we were coming to live in France permanently, had just arrived, that a transport company was bringing all our furniture, and that we had brought the cat, with its papers, and were supposed to declare it. The lorry driver stared at us both as if nobody but lunatics would take a cat from one country to another, but said nothing.

'Je suis anglais,' I said, for no particular reason except that I had already realised in our various dealings over the purchase of the house that in the French mind it is a formula which accounts for a good deal of odd behaviour.

'Ah, bon,' said Monsieur Charles, lighting a Gauloise, and moving behind the desk, next to Albert. 'Let's have a look.' He scanned through the papers. 'No problem,' he said to Albert. 'Sign here. And here. That's it, then. Voilà, c'est tout.'

'Really?' Albert's relief was undisguised. 'Thank you, monsieur Charles. But, but what about all this?'

'Nothing to do with you, petit. All that is for Périgueux. You have nothing to do there. These people can go now.'

'Merci, monsieur Charles.'

'De rien. Mes salutations à votre maman.'

'Les miens aussi,' added his friend.

'Au revoir, monsieur, dame. Bonne journée, bon voyage, et bon séjour en France.'

So we drove off, heading south, with one cat with her papers in order.

And now here we were, waiting. The cat had disappeared, the furniture van had at the very least gone wildly astray, and we were beginning to feel both despondent and hungry. We waited and the hours went by. It began to rain and it was unseasonably cold, and we began to notice it. M. Rambaud had left us an antique central heating system but no fuel oil.

At four o'clock I decided to go looking for the van.

'What good will that do? He could be anywhere. In a ditch with all our furniture.'

I could see the picture she had in mind. The van on its side. The driver on his back, surrounded by beds, chairs, blankets and saucepans. A country gendarme scratching his head and looking round for help.

'I'll go anyway. You never know. I won't be long. Just round about here.'

I drove out and turned right. After about four hundred metres the road forks, left to the four houses and the church that form our local hamlet, right to a single track bridge. I could not turn left, and I could not stop because there was a French car following one metre behind mine, a situation I have since become used to. I desperately wanted to stop because the reason I could not turn left was that the entrance to that road was blocked by a huge furniture van. The road to the bridge runs along a narrow embankment with a sharp drop on either side. I slowed down although it was virtually impossible to turn round even if I could stop, but I immediately got a blast on the horn from the driver behind. Nothing for it but to carry on across the bridge, where on the other side the road forked again and there was room to turn round, and come back and hope the van was still there.

It was, and the driver, who had obviously been asking his way from a man on a bicycle, was getting back into his cab.

'Sorry I could not help you,' the bike man was saying. 'Don't know of any such house near here. Tell you what though, there's another Solignac in Dordogne.'

'How far's that, then?' asked the driver, in passable French.

'Must be about a hundred kilometres.'

'No, no,' I shouted, having parked the car precariously on the edge of the embankment. 'Don't go. If you are looking for St Pierre de Dantou, it's just down the road, only about four hundred metres.'

He held a piece of paper out to me. 'This you then?'

'Yes, yes. Follow me.'

'Thank the effing stars for that. Sorry I'm late, mate. Got trapped in a blizzard in the mountains.'

Mountains? I drove off, and he followed, and somehow got the van into our narrow drive and to the front of the house. Marie-Anne was waiting.

'Bonjour, monsieur,' she said to the driver, and 'What happened?' to me.

'Says he got snowed up in the mountains.'

'Mountains? There are no mountains on the way here.'

'Depends how you come, missus. We had another load to deliver on the way, near Vichy. Got that off all right, then this muck-up in the Massif Central. 'Orrible place this time of year.'

'Well, thank goodness you've arrived at last. I was giving up hope.'

'Better show us where you want it all. Not that we'll get it all off tonight, but we might as well start.' He went round to the back and opened the doors, justifying his use of the royal 'we', as another man in overalls emerged, stretching.

It seemed they had hardly started, when it became too dark to see what they were doing. In a moment of weakness M. Rambaud had left us two light bulbs, one of which worked. It was hardly enough, so when the foreman said, 'Fixed up for tonight, are you?' we took the hint. We were tired and, now that we knew we had some furniture as well as a house, our hopes and appetites had returned, so we agreed to call it a day, and start again in the morning. We went back to our hotel and had a good dinner.

In the morning we drove early to the house. The men were already there, watching the fish in the little ornamental pond, while they waited to start. No doubt M. Rambaud would have liked to take the fish with him but, as we discovered later, the only way to get goldfish out of a pond is to empty it and then pick them up by hand. The men worked non-stop, not even wanting to break for lunch. I went to the village and brought back bottled beer and ham sandwiches, French variety, each about a foot long, which they ate in between hefting things from the van to the house.

By the end of the afternoon, the van was empty and the house was full. Everything we had sent had arrived safely and been unloaded without incident. The waiting and the suspense had been forgotten.

They were admirable men. They took blizzards in their stride, if rather slowly, and they had lost nothing, and broken nothing. At least, I am reasonably sure that they hadn't . . . That was in March 1983, and there are still two unopened cartons in the attic. I don't know what is inside them, and whatever it is it may be broken, but I doubt if it matters now. They told me what they were at the time, but I have forgotten. Everything was marked with a code they understood, so that whenever Marie-Anne said things like 'What has happened to my dinner service?' They would reply with 'What room was it in in London – basement kitchen?' and walk up to a carton: 'There you are then, basement kitchen – no, not that one, that's cooking utensils. Here you are, dinner service, thirty-three pieces.'

We opened a few to test their assertions, and they were always right, so we just checked the unopened cartons against our list, and when everything was unloaded and we had checked through it with them, we signed.

'Nice place you've got here,' said one. 'Lot of work, though.' It was the understated prophecy of the year.

'No Indian shop round the corner,' said the other, thinking of London.

'Right then, we'll be off.'

We gave them more beer and sandwiches for the journey, and thanked them.

'You 'ave been marvellous,' said Marie-Anne, with a charming smile and the French accent which thirty years in England had done nothing to change.

They smiled back. 'All in the day's. Good luck, then.' The van lumbered off to the north, and we turned back into the chaos of the house to start a different life.

Chapter Two

A White House in the Sun

The house we had bought had been at some time a typical Gascon farmhouse, consisting of a ground floor inhabited by the farmer and his family, and an upper storey with two spacious attics, called 'greniers', which originally were used for storing bales of fodder for the cattle in winter, but it was a long time since the house had seen a farmer. What it had seen was a succession of bizarre owners, culminating in M. Rambaud, each of whom had tarted it up in his own way. In this part of France successful farmers never felt the necessity to consult an architect when deciding to build or enlarge a house. They began by following the usual pattern, a wide central hall from back to front with two large rooms on each side. If they had money to spare, they would indulge their particular fancies here and there, usually towers, turrets or castellations.

According to M. Rambaud, who seemed to find life dull and in need of constant embellishment, our house had been built during the French Revolution, an assertion which the lawyer who dealt with the transaction met with a shrug and 'It's possible'. Well, it sounded interesting and who could prove otherwise? When we knew M. Rambaud better we were surprised that he had not claimed that it was the Scarlet Pimpernel's country hideaway.

The house had four downstairs rooms, each about sixteen feet square. The first bathroom had been put in, something like a hundred and eighty years after the house was built, by a retired dancer from the Moulin Rouge, installed there as mistress of a heavily married Bergerac wine merchant, who wanted her at a safe distance. There had been a single-storey lean-to pigsty on one side of the house. What she had done was to make it half bathroom, half kitchen. The original short, high-sided iron bath was still there, perched on its toes like a four-legged ballet dancer, together with a splendid rectangular hand-basin not much smaller than the bath, a bidet and a loo with an orange plastic cover, with a brush container to match. These last M. Rambaud kindly offered to leave us, and he kept his word.

Two of the downstairs rooms had been used as bedrooms, and each had a floor-to-ceiling cupboard of impressive proportions, not quite large enough to play a hand of cards in, but large enough for the dancer to have turned them into what the French call 'cabinets de toilette', each with tiny triangular wash-basins and towel racks. After this she ran out of ideas, but being an active lady with time on her hands, and Bergerac being forty miles away and the wine merchant's visits at boringly long intervals, she struck up a friendly relationship with the mayor of a nearby village.

Nothing stays secret for long in the country. The Bergerac wine merchant was soon au fait with the turn of events, and the house was sold.

The new owners were 'pieds noirs' – 'black feet', as the French in mainland France call the French who were born and brought up in Algeria, which was French for well over a hundred years. When President de Gaulle returned Algeria to the Algerians, thousands of French came from Algeria to France, obliged to leave their land and possessions behind. We never knew whether the awful kitchen was the work of the enterprising lady from Paris or the 'black feet', or possibly M. Rambaud himself. It contained a wood-burning range with marble panels behind it which appeared to have been taken from a tomb, an antique gas stove, preserved in grease, and fitted metal cupboards painted white.

'This will have to go,' said Marie-Anne.

'What?'

'All of it.'

I did not argue. Thirty years' experience had taught me that it was as good as gone. Marie-Anne is the kindest and most gentle of women, but stubborn. In any case I was in complete agreement with her, though I was feeling the first of a long series of financial aches and pains.

So that was the ground floor: four large rooms, a spacious

central hall, plus a kitchen and bathroom area, already condemned. Beneath the whole of one side of the house there was a huge cellar, large enough for a billiard room, a laundry, or just to store enough wine for a Roman orgy. Unfortunately the boiler and the fuel storage tanks had been placed more or less in the middle. The warmth of the boiler spoiled it as a wine cellar, and the storage tanks have so far proved an insurmountable barrier to other uses. In one corner there was a bed of earth about a foot deep contained by a low brick wall. It could have been a grave, and I have preferred not to investigate it, but M. Rambaud claimed that he had successfully cultivated mushrooms there, and in view of his known eccentricities, I think he probably did try.

A part of the wall adjacent to the mushroom bed appeared to be made from different stones from the rest. It was the shape of a small door. I pointed it out to M. Rambaud.

'Ah, well. There was a lot of religious persecution at the time of the Revolution, and the people in this part of France were very religious, many of them Huguenots,' he said, and at least that part was true. 'There were many places where the priests could hide, and this is one of them. There was a door here, and behind the door a tunnel which led to a cave on the river bank. The priest could hide there for days, if necessary. No doubt the tunnel has collapsed but the cave is still there.'

That bit was also true. There is a cave, now well hidden by trailing vegetation, in the steep river bank. I have not explored it for signs of a tunnel, and I don't think I'll bother.

This cellar has an outside door which is approached down a slope excavated at some time in the past at the side of the house. The wall in which the door is set is five feet thick, and the oak door has been adorned on the outside by M. Rambaud with an enamel sign, perhaps 'acquired' from the local electricity board, of a white skull and crossbones on a red background with the words 'Danger de Mort' underneath. He said he felt that it was a deterrent. Inside the house a door beneath the staircase opens on to a flight of ancient stone steps leading down. I hope one day to be able to negotiate them without hitting my head on the cross-beam. Even today, Gascon peasants are not very tall, and at the time of the French Revolution they must have been a lot smaller.

In barns, outhouses, attics and cellars, one metre sixty (five foot three inches) is a generous height for a door, so one thing I have found essential for living on a French farm is a thick skull. I learned this the hard way, very early on, when I showed a new delivery man where to fill the fuel oil tanks. In this operation the 'Danger de Mort' door is opened and the pipe from the tanker is brought down the slope and into the cellar. He put the nozzle in the tank, switched on, and then went back to the tanker lorry, saying he'd be back at once. He wasn't and the tank started to overflow. In my haste to warn him I dashed to the door and ran my head full tilt into the stone lintel. I saw stars, and fell flat on my back in the spilled oil, but eventually got away with seven stitches in my scalp. I was lucky. Except that he was chasing a serving maid not a delivery man, King Charles VIII of France did exactly the same thing and died from a fractured skull. I have banged my head on low doorways several times since, but never again that particular one.

The first floor is still much as we found it, with the two large attics, running from back to front of the house. Space had been taken from one of them to make a bathroom somewhat less medieval than the one downstairs. The other was its full thirty-four by sixteen feet. The wall was in the natural stone. It had never been plastered, and here and there a large chunk of rock protruded several inches into the room from the otherwise level surface, and I wondered why. M. Rambaud for once had nothing to say, but I learned much later from one of the masons that these very large stones ran through the thickness of the wall to strengthen it, and because of the weight and the labour involved, the mason was rewarded with a litre of wine for each one he put in position.

There was a small, deep recess in this wall near one corner, and M. Rambaud did have something to say about that. According to him, there had been a small window there, now bricked up, where some previous owners, engaged in the smuggling trade, had placed a lantern as a signal to men who brought the goods up river. There was no shred of evidence for the truth of this, though it was just possible. There had at one time been a considerable river trade between Libourne and Cahors. Boats called 'gabarres' brought stockfish – sun-dried cod or haddock – to Cahors as a cheap food, taking back with them Cahors wines destined for England, and no doubt some smuggling went on as well. Every summer a week of motor-boat races and other events on the river Lot, called 'La route du vin et du stockfish', commemorates those times.

Between the two attics, over the front two-thirds of the hall, M. Rambaud had installed what he described as a 'chambre d'hôte', a guest bedroom. As with most of his ideas, the conception was considerably grander than the execution. Although it was done as cheaply as possible, it is nevertheless a pleasant room. One of M. Rambaud's whimsicalities was to make the house look as much like the White House in Washington as possible. The fact that it was a great deal smaller and he had no intention of spending the money to bring it up to scratch in no way deterred him. What he did was to add a porch with pillars, flanked by a balustrade along the front of the house, and a pediment to break the roof line. Each of the rooms at the front had French windows opening on to the garden, and these were also framed with pillars and given a pediment. The porch is square not semi-circular, and its flat roof is enclosed in a balustrade to match that at ground level. The charm of the guest bedroom is that it has a double French door leading on to the flat roof, which makes an excellent balcony with plenty of room for a breakfast table and chairs.

M. Rambaud was proud of all this. 'The peasants call it the White House,' he said. But the 'peasants' put it differently. 'He calls it the White House,' they said. The overall effect was of something vaguely Georgian, designed in an alcoholic haze. But M. Rambaud, for his health's sake, was a teetotaller. Anyway, the result was quite pleasing once we had simplified it.

When peasants in this part of France began to farm a new piece of land two hundred years ago or more, the first thing they did was to put up a small single-storey building, usually just a living room and a bedroom, in which they lived while they got the land into shape. Once this had been done, they built the farmhouse proper and moved into it, and the farmer would install a labourer in the original house. Many of these small houses still exist and are known as 'fermettes', 'little farms'. Ours was still there a few yards to the west of the main house. It had been extended by a 'chai', a room for storing wine, and another room containing a prune oven, both of which were falling down, and a further extension, about seven feet by twelve, containing a stone sink and a ruined shower. M. Rambaud described this extension as 'the chauffeur's room', and we later found a key to it with a label so marked.

We had been told that when M. Rambaud first arrived – he had been there about twenty years – he did indeed have a large American limousine, and a rapid succession of chauffeurs. None of them stayed long, because having used it two or three times to impress the neighbourhood, M. Rambaud, who did not himself drive, had the limousine put in the barn, and refused to license or insure it. The chauffeurs got tired of polishing a car they could not drive, and of being asked to grow vegetables instead, and left one after the other. M. Rambaud gave up the pretence and sold the car.

Next to the fermette there is a really lovely old barn, built at about the same time as the main house, with a wonderful frame-work of oak and elm beams, cut straight from the tree by hand, and still intact. Or so we thought. Like all the traditional barns in Gascony it had an open but roofed overhang or canopy, called an 'auvent', about twenty feet deep and the full width of the barn. From the main cross-beam of this auvent a magnificent vine, a kind of Virginia creeper, hung like a natural curtain. Its flaming colours in autumn gave us a lot of pleasure for two or three years, until the whole thing fell down one Sunday afternoon.

But that was only one of several disasters which we suffered in fairly rapid succession, and it was not the first. Together they made us feel, especially when considered in conjunction with the state of the house, which gradually showed itself to be much more shabby and fatigued than we had thought, that perhaps M. Rambaud had included hypnotism among his other unusual qualities. But then we remembered that, despite the fact that we were relatively experienced in property, having bought, restored and sold several houses and flats, and knowing perfectly well how important a sound survey is, we decided without hesitation not to have one done. The only explanation for this was that we knew, of course, that heads would wag, and we would be told what a mess it was, and not to touch it at any price, and it would cost a fortune to restore, et cetera. We did not wish to be dissuaded. We even paid over the odds for the house, and M. Rambaud went off proud and happy, convinced that he was one of life's great swindlers.

On the face of things it seemed that we were mad, and the local population, that is the farmers on either side, were convinced – and remain convinced – that we had more money than we knew what to do with, which was certainly a long way from the truth. As to our joint sanity, I can only say that in the years that we have been here some hundreds of people have stayed in the two holiday cottages which we managed to make from the picturesque ruins on either side of the farmhouse, and that, summed up, their shared opinion has been 'What a lovely place.'

Why? The answer has nothing to do with the particular cottages, or any other single aspect of the property. From the outside it all looks essentially the same as it did, a bit cleaner and tidier, that's all. But some houses and their setting, like some people, have an underlying harmony that makes them attractive. If a beautiful woman puts on old clothes and doesn't bother to comb her hair, her beauty is still there, and some people will see it. The same thing applies to houses, even to places. A house can be neglected, in disrepair, the garden overgrown, but the proportions and the essential setting are still there, waiting to be recognised. Perhaps it is this quality of rightness and harmony that people find in our 'farm', and that Marie-Anne and I were lucky enough to see. Perhaps in a way M. Rambaud had felt it himself and his attempts at improvements sprang from this, but when he tried to sell it the local people were not interested. They saw only an old farmhouse that was no longer the standard for the region, and were therefore unable to judge its value, and on top of that they did not trust M. Rambaud.

But the place as a whole, considered objectively, does have charm. It lies between a by-road and the bank of the river Lot. You approach it down a hundred-metre drive, avenue is too grand a word, lined by tall cedars. Behind the cedars on the right-hand side is a row of twenty apple trees, Golden Delicious and others, and beyond that an orchard of plum trees. On the left-hand side behind the cedars is a row of twenty pear trees, some of them Williams, and beyond that, when we arrived, was an ancient plum orchard, full of gaps and dying trees, so that on a wet day it looked like an illustration of a World War I battlefield.

At the end of the drive there is a gateway with two old stone pillars. There was also, I discovered, under the vegetation which grew around them, a gate which appeared to have been made from gas piping, and was hanging off its hinges. Eventually, with a few iron bars and some chicken wire added, it made an excellent reinforcement for a concrete landing stage which we built beside the river. The gateway is arched over by two old tamarisk trees covered in pink blossom every spring. The drive continues in a curve past the front of the barn and then curves again and crosses the front of the house at right angles to the barn. It then swings round to the left and rejoins itself outside the gateway, so that a car can be driven in, to the house, and out again without having to reverse.

The space in front of the house and the barn, enclosed by the drive, forms a garden about forty metres square. When we moved in, this space was occupied by a weed-infested lawn, which M. Rambaud described as informal, surrounding the ornamental pond. The two sides opposite the house and the barn were enclosed by what had once been a cypress hedge, grown after fifteen years of neglect into trees about twenty-five feet tall, creating a gloomy effect. But nature, as we soon discovered, often has something up her sleeve in this part of France, and was to take a hand in re-landscaping this part of the property.

Behind the house, between it and the river, there is another plum orchard. Marie-Anne wanted an 'orchard' of her own, so we took a corner of this and I planted six peach trees, three white, three yellow, and a couple of cherries. The river cannot be seen from the house or the orchard, as the bank is about thirty feet high. From the edge of the plum orchard you go down to the waterside by a broad path which descends the bank in an easy zigzag through a plantation of mature poplars, interspersed with acacias and a walnut. In spring the acacias are covered in a very sweetly scented white blossom, and on warm days the perfume drifts on the breeze all round the house. The local farmers' wives pick the blossom and use it to flavour small pancakes.

There is another garden behind the barn and the fermette. It contained, when we arrived, a very large L-shaped concreted hole in the ground. It was difficult to judge what it was, because it was almost completely overhung by cedars and cypresses, and the bottom was thick with the accumulation of years of leaves, twigs and pine needles, but M. Rambaud said it was a swimming pool. He produced snapshots showing people in the water. The trees surrounding the pool were little more than saplings, indicating that the pictures must have been taken at least fifteen years earlier.

There was no filtration system, he said. He used to ask the neighbouring farmer to fill the pool from the river through irrigation pipes and then added some chemicals. From the old photographs the resulting water was an interesting yellow-brown colour. It was some years since it had been used, he said. Whether it still held water was anybody's guess, but we noted that M. Rambaud made no confident assertions that it did. It was a chance we would have to take.

So that was the property, house, barn, fermette, pigeon-house, garden, query swimming pool, a couple of viable plum orchards and one which looked like a battlefield, a cereal field, a river bank with a light wood of poplars. Nothing on a large scale, and about ten acres in all. Nothing in good condition, some of it decrepit. And yet ... And yet, there was no doubt that once restored it would be very pleasant indeed. But where to begin?

Chapter Three

ART LOVER AND CON MAN

The formalities of buying a house in France are in some ways simpler than in England. The legalities are dealt with by a 'notaire', who, as far as property transactions are concerned, is a government agent, and so acts impartially for both buyer and seller. There are no long-winded exchanges of letters between solicitors on both sides.

The notaire we dealt with, M. de Moulin, was an island of calm and sanity between the undoubtedly eccentric M. Rambaud and the completely different but equally curious M. Morgan, the estate agent. Looking back, all they had in common was the ability to spot what con men used to call a 'pigeon'. M. Morgan, despite his name, was a Gascon, descended no doubt, like the occasional Browns and Robinsons found in the Bordeaux region, from some gallant British soldier of the Hundred Years War. Dealing with M. Morgan was something of a riot. In the first place his accent was so strong that Marie-Anne, although French herself, said to me after our first meeting with him, 'I can hardly understand him. I think he must be Greek. Perhaps his name is really Morganides or Morganopoulos, or something like that.' I don't know whether some echo from her classical education had told her subconscious to beware of Greeks bearing gifts, and was relating this to M. Morgan's insistence that the house was a give-away at the price. The second thing about M. Morgan was that he was as deaf as a doorknob. He wore an old-fashioned hearing aid which he often took out and fiddled with, but whatever he did, he succeeded only in hearing what he wanted to hear. His answers to our questions consisted of statements praising some aspect of the property which he thought would please us, and rarely had much to do with the question. When we asked about the water supply, he told us how many tons of plums the orchards produced and no they didn't like a lot of water. It was all a bit like the old men on the London bus – Is this Wembley? No, Thursday. So am I, let's have a drink.

When he took us to meet M. Rambaud for the first time and showed us around the property, we did notice that he seemed to hear M. Rambaud a great deal better than he did us. I did not expect him to understand my Franglais and, in fact, after watching me carefully when I spoke for the first time, he thereafter ignored everything I said and concentrated on Marie-Anne. In fact, on the site he left the talking to M. Rambaud, and ambled happily through the orchard, munching plums. It was towards the end of August and the trees were heavy with juicy, purple fruit for which M. Morgan seemed to have an unlimited capacity.

M. Rambaud tried hard to sell his property, even proposing an unfamiliar method of purchase called a 'viager libre', which consists of a down payment, called a 'bouquet', followed by a life annuity to the seller. The amounts involved depend very much on the age and state of health of the seller. Someone in their sixties is likely to get much less than a ninety-year-old with chronic bronchitis. The risks are not all with the buyer. Several films have been made concerning the premature deaths of sellers whose 'viager' seemed to be going on too long. During this discussion M. Rambaud did his best to convince us that he had one foot in the grave; every now and then he would wince discreetly and press a hand to his side, and it was noticeable that when we had persuaded him that we were really not interested in that method, his pains disappeared.

It was the second property which we had looked at, and on that first visit they failed to convince us. We went away and over the next two or three months and a couple more trips, looked at different properties of all kinds, about thirty altogether. Some we liked, and almost all of them were cheaper and would have been a great deal less trouble, but they were what they were, with little room for improvement, and selfishly I wanted something to do.

So we went back to M. Morgan. We realised almost at once that it was a mistake. The best tactics would have been to treat M. Rambaud like a dealer in an Oriental bazaar, to laugh at his asking price and walk away, and keep on with the same attitude until he saw reason. Having decided that M. Rambaud's house was the one that interested us we should have contrived to meet M. Morgan 'by accident' and have let him know casually that we were still looking and, perhaps, M. Rambaud's might have interested us, just possibly, had the price been a fair one. It might have worked but we have since found out that there is a kind of Frenchman who is happy to sell provided he can get an exaggerated price, and who has no intention of ever selling at a fair price. Perhaps we felt instinctively that M. Rambaud had romantically set a price to match what he sometimes ennobled to his 'country manor' and once, even, his 'little château', and would rather starve than lose face by selling below it.

Once we were installed and knew our neighbouring farmers, we learned that M. Rambaud had gradually drifted down to the level where he relied very strongly for food on what he grew himself which, apart from fruit, was very little. There was no sign of a vegetable garden when we took over. The farmers considered him helpless, and would out of pity give him vegetables, when he bought half a dozen eggs from them once a week.

M. Rambaud had, in fact, never done a day's work in his life. He described himself as a dilettante and lover of the arts. He was not a Gascon; he came originally from Alsace, where his father owned a factory making chamber pots – until recent years, in the frequent absence of inside loos or bathrooms, still much in use in France – and other basic china. As a boy during World War II he had been sent for safety to a relative in Dordogne, where he went to school. His father died when M. Rambaud was still a young man, and he had lived ever since on the capital which he had inherited.

When the capital began to decline, M. Rambaud felt obliged to get married. Since he was by preference homosexual, it might have been supposed that this step would present difficulties, but he succeeded in marrying someone who was not only younger than himself, but who belonged to a rich family whose food products were and are a household name in France. Not only that, according to local gossip, his current boyfriend accompanied the newly-weds on their honeymoon.

The marriage was not a success but it stumbled on for a number of years during which Madame Rambaud's money enabled them to live in comfort. Mme Rambaud was a trained and talented painter with a high degree of technical skill. It seemed to M. Rambaud that it would be a tragedy to waste such a gift, and he somehow persuaded his wife that it would be nice to have some copies of works by famous artists, just as decoration. They would go very nicely with the antique furniture which she had been given by her mother, and other relatives, as wedding presents.

One day Mme Rambaud, who had just returned from a visit to her family in Paris, was walking through the streets of a local town when a rather fine antique sideboard in the window of a furniture shop caught her eye. It looked, she thought, very like her sideboard. And on the wall to the right of it was a painting, which also seemed familiar. To cut a long story short, Mme Rambaud had been tightening the purse strings and M. Rambaud had taken advantage of her absence to augment his income. How they sorted it out between them I don't know, but some time after we moved in we met Mme Rambaud through a mutual friend, and she told us this and other stories over dinner. According to her, she enjoyed copying the occasional Van Gogh or Vermeer and found it helped her to develop her own skills, but she was interested only in her own original paintings, and took no interest in what happened to the copies after she had finished them. However she did know of a dentist, and a couple of local shops, who had accepted them from M. Rambaud in settlement of accounts. She was not surprised to learn that her ex-husband had asked us if we would be interested in buying a painting by Ingres, which he said had been in the Dordogne branch of the family for generations. Her husband liked her to do an Ingres occasionally, she said, because he was an artist of the south-west, having lived and worked in Montauban, between Agen and Toulouse. Fortunately, I neither liked nor could afford the picture.

But M. Rambaud was nothing if not versatile. He was, as he had told us, a lover of the arts, particularly music. He had been a talented violinist in his youth, he said, and had at one time considered becoming a professional. The conversation turned to music a few days after I had failed to show any enthusiasm for the Ingres. He had been obliged to give up playing because of arthritis in his hands but in his youth had shown so much talent, he said, that his father – 'It was in the days when the family had real money, you understand' – had made him a present of a Stradivarius. Alas, he had not touched it for years, and would never play it again. But in preparing for his departure he had come across it and wondered whether perhaps I would like to buy it. Even after thirty years it must be worth a thousand or two, he added, gracefully implying that he was as ignorant as he hoped I was. It looked a fine old instrument, and he pointed out the various signs and labels indicating that it was indeed, apparently, a Stradivarius.

I can see now that having labelled myself a mug in capital letters, as far as he was concerned, by agreeing to pay his inflated price for the house, M. Rambaud felt it was well worth a try. He was not to know that by pure chance I knew somebody in one of the very few shops in the world where you could sometimes walk in and buy a real Stradivarius. Years before I had written an article about this shop and the wonderful musical instruments that could be bought there and the famous musicians who were its customers. I telephoned them and told them the story. My contact did not appear to be over-excited. 'Have a look at it and check these three points. If the answer is "yes" in each case, it will be one of two or three thousand fakes made in Bavaria about sixty years ago. Quite nice little instruments really, worth about fifty pounds today in perfect condition.' The answers, of course, were in the affirmative, so I do not have a Stradivarius. I did not say anything to M. Rambaud about expert opinions; for all I know he believed it really was a Stradivarius, though I hardly think it is likely. I just declined his offer.

So the preliminaries leading to the house purchase were not without interest, although, so to speak, we lost every round. I have already mentioned the stone baskets of fruit, ancient and sculpted, which M. Rambaud promised to leave and didn't. There was also a nice old trap (no pony), in reasonable condition which he said he would include in the price, but which disappeared before we moved in. He did leave the orange plastic loo equipment which looked like a fairground booby prize, and he did leave a two-stroke lawn-mower which, once it had been started, worked perfectly well for five minutes and then gave up for that day. At intervals over several years I and various odd-job men, garage mechanics and lawn-mower specialists tried to persuade it to do better. Eventually one naive young man, instead of charging for a fictional repair, explained to me carefully why it was fit only for the scrapheap. And M. Rambaud would happily have left us a large and cumbersome piece of agricultural machinery, a harrow I think it was, which should have been in an agricultural museum. We had to remind him several times that he had said he would dispose of it, and tell him that we had spoken to the notaire about it, but in the end he did get rid of it.

The moral of all this is that if you are buying a property in France, and there is something you particularly want, or do not want, to be included in the sale, inform the notaire and get it in writing. If you do not, you may get an unpleasant surprise. A Mr and Mrs Coghill, a charming Irish couple, who arrived here after us, decided recently that their house was too isolated, and Mrs Coghill wanted to be closer to her children, who live in Somerset. She found a house she liked in Normandy not far from the coast, and they bought it. She had been particularly impressed with the modern fitted kitchen, and was outraged when she moved in to find that the previous owner had not only taken everything that was removable, including every light switch and bulb except one, but also the whole of the fitted kitchen. Not a shelf or a cupboard remained, just the bare walls. She had not thought it necessary to make it clear to the notaire that the fitted kitchen was to be included in the price.

As in England, estate agents in France work to a set scale of fees which varies according to the value of the property sold, and which is or should be on view somewhere in their office. Look in a gloomy corner. However, in some administrative areas the estate agent's fee is paid by the vendor, not the buyer, and this is a point worth checking as soon as you start looking for a property.

All buying and selling of property in France has to take into consideration the dreamier aspects of the French character. They think of themselves as tough and down to earth, but they are fantasists. Whatever they may tell you, they are much less realistic than the British. They are obsessed with winning a fortune. They dream of winning the Loto, or the Tac-o-Tac or the Tapis Vert, three government-controlled gambling games, or the daily horse-racing triple, quadruple or quintuple bets on the PariMutuel, the French equivalent of the Tote, or one of the countless television gambling games with prizes of up to ten thousand pounds a night, or one of the innumerable prizes offered on packets of cereal, washing-up liquid or tins of beans. And they dream of selling their house for far more than it is worth. An acquaintance of mine who sells nothing but châteaux told me categorically that the average French owner putting his property up for sale overestimates its value by at least 20 per cent, and will stick out for years for his asking price, refusing offers that come quite close to it, when he could have made a sale after a short time and put his money to work to earn the difference. The same sort of owner often likes to say that his is the best house, farm, château or whatever in the area, brushing aside the fact that foreigners, retired people, and many other buyers are not obliged to go to any particular place, and will simply look for something similar but better value somewhere else.

It is important to get value for money with the bricks and mortar, if you can, but a house is always more than just that. We had bought more than a property, we had bought a new life in a different country, a life full of new interests, new problems, fresh faces, challenges of all kinds. We thought then, and we still think, that it was not such a bad deal.

Chapter Four

THE PIGEON-HOUSE GANG

The problem was, what to do exactly? Having been the travel editor of a national newspaper, I had learned by association something about the tourist industry. I knew, for example, that a good campsite, particularly when you kept the management in your own hands, could be the source of a considerable income. We had the land, but did we have the inclination? We decided that the answer was 'no', mainly because it was impossible to site it far enough away from the house which was going to be our permanent home, but also because it would be time-consuming and involve too much work.

On the other hand self-catering cottages for holidaymakers would, once established, be very little trouble, we thought. But how many of these 'gîtes ruraux', as they are called in France, should we have? There seemed to be room for three or four on the edges of the orchards, and for another half a dozen spread along the river bank.

'How about one?' said Marie-Anne. 'We'll start with the "pigeonnier", and see how we go.'

Dreamer I may be, but I have a practical side and I gave in without a struggle to the common sense behind this remark. These pigeonniers, or pigeon-houses, are separate buildings, usually two storeys high with a steeply pitched roof. They exist in other parts of France – there are some very fine examples in Normandy – but they are a typical feature of the farms throughout Gascony. Some of them contained many hundreds of birds, which were kept both as a source of food and for the fertiliser which they provided. Ours was larger than most, about five metres square inside.

Not surprisingly, M. Rambaud's version of the uses to which a pigeonnier should be put had differed considerably from the norm. At some time a single-storey lean-to building had been added on the side away from the main house. It had solid walls and a tiled roof but no windows; light was admitted through a door made of battens and chicken wire. The lean-to had once been used as a poultry shed and the area in front of it, enclosed by chain-link fencing and roofed by a net, as a chicken run, but not by M. Rambaud. He had used it as an aviary for exotic birds, including peacocks, and several kinds of rare pheasants. Within the enclosure, against the wall of the pigeonnier, there was another structure with a raised floor and several tiers of hutches above, in which he had bred angora rabbits.

Our daughter Ari, who arrived a few days after we moved in, curious to see what her parents had encumbered themselves with, joined in our daily search for the cat. Cleo, who was really hers, had not reappeared since dashing off when she was let out of the car on arrival. For some reason Ari thought of looking under the raised floor of the rabbit house and, in the darkest and furthest corner, she spotted a pair of eyes staring out at her. Cleo, who must have been getting pretty hungry, was easily enticed out with a saucer of milk, and from that day on began to explore the property.

Apart from the poultry shed, the rabbit house and the exotic aviary, there were other problems with the pigeonnier. The only way into the main part was by a very attractive pair of arched French windows about eight feet wide. Mme Rambaud had made her studio on the ground floor of the pigeonnier, and as painters prefer a north light, she had replaced the original five-foot farm door by this lovely double window. She had a north light certainly, but the only view was of the white wall of the side of the main house twenty feet away. What had been her studio would have to be the living room, and a holiday cottage with a living room in which guests could see nothing but a blank wall, when it was surrounded on its other three sides by country views and vegetation, was out of the question.

Another problem was that there was no way up from the ground floor to the actual pigeon-loft except by a rickety ladder which Mme Rambaud had installed, so that she could climb up there to nail her various Rembrandts, Van Goghs, Gauguins and her own paintings, of course, to the rafters to dry. A staircase would be needed. The wooden floor of the loft, though it had been quite safe for pigeons for a couple of hundred years and, apparently, for the light and bird-like Mme Rambaud, would clearly not be strong enough for bedroom furniture, plus tourist couples whose combined weight might be two or three times that of Mme Rambaud. We did not want anyone to fall through the floor on holiday, so we would have to reinforce it.

The lean-to was amply big enough to convert to a kitchen and a bathroom, though pigeons, of course, are well known for their lack of concern for such things as toilets and drains, and these were missing. Thinking things over I was beginning to believe the Job's comforters who had warned me that restoring old properties was more expensive than building new ones. Happily, this turned out to be some way from the truth, even in the case of the pigeonnier, over which we, as ingenuous innocents, were, to put it gently, taken advantage of.

We had mentioned to M. Rambaud and to M. Morgan, and to our neighbours, that we thought of having cottages for tourists. This caused a certain amount of polite laughter, and some more open hilarity, all round. It is true that in 1983 there were no tourism development committees in the department. Agriculture was all-important and tourism was hardly ever mentioned in the local papers. M. Morgan, however, did not laugh, except perhaps up his sleeve. He appeared to take our ideas very seriously, and said he knew exactly the man to carry them out just as we wanted, a M. Bellin. It was not until after we had agreed, and the work was started, that we discovered that M. Bellin happened to be M. Morgan's son-in-law.

We realised then that we were not likely to be undercharged for the work to be done, but we had not had time to get to know any of the local craftsmen, and we felt that M. Bellin and his team would get the conversion done much more quickly than we would be able to by trial and error among the different artisans.

There are three ways of restoring old property in France. First, you can do it all yourself, if you have the skills, or are prepared to acquire them. You also need a lot of time.

The second method is to employ local artisans yourself. This can be slow because they all work independently, and things have to be done in the right order and you may be ready for the next workman long before he is ready for you. A neighbour of mine employed a cabinet maker to convert a room to a home office. The man did some of the work, but left the necessary bookcase and filing system. It was a year before he came back and finished it. That is an extreme case, but there are bound to be delays with this second system. It is, however, much the cheapest way, especially if you can do some of the work yourself, and if you are careful to ask for at least three different estimates for each job to be done. The difference between them can be astonishing, hundreds of pounds on the more important jobs. We had several in which the cheapest was less than half the most expensive.

One of the unfamiliar things in France is that there are no jobbing builders, each with his own team of workmen. Instead, there are 'maîtres d'oeuvres'; the English equivalent of this is 'clerks of works' but in Britain such men are usually in somebody's employ, whereas in France they are independent. They know numbers of artisans in different fields, and when they get a job, they create a team, according to who is free at the time. The maître d'oeuvres is, therefore, providing work for them, and in return he takes a percentage of the value of the work done. The workmen do not work for less than they would do on a job obtained independently so, of course, they add the maître d'oeuvres' fee to what they charge the client. The extra that the client pays can be seen, if you like, as a premium for getting the work done without delay.

This, then, is the third method, to employ a maître d'oeuvres such as M. Bellin and leave it all to him, and this is what we did for the restoration of the pigeonnier. It cost more than it need have done, but watching the work, and asking questions, amounted to a free course in the restoration of old buildings and taught us a great deal, which we have since used to advantage.

It was an interesting experience in another way. We had often worked with builders in England, both in the country and in central London. None of them, as we recalled, had seemed in anyway unusual. The only possible exception was an aged and truculent plumber known throughout our part of Westminster as 'Ernie'. He looked like an undersized jockey, and always wore a dusty, brown trilby hat. He was apparently, worth his weight – which was not much – in gold, for his ability to get into the almost inaccessible corners of ancient buildings.

When I saw M. Bienvenue, the plumber of what we soon called the Pigeonnier Gang, I thought at once of Ernie, and felt they would have recognised each other on sight. M. Bienvenue was a little taller but equally insubstantial. He appeared to consist entirely of a pair of ancient blue overalls and a cap, which he never took off.

The rest of the gang that M. Bellin put together were as varied as their trades. Perhaps it was only that it was our first experience of French workmen, and that they were not just foreigners, but 'foreign' foreigners, but most of them seemed to us to be out of the ordinary. The masons, for example, were of Italian descent, born in France but of parents who had disagreed with Mussolini without stopping to argue with him. Instead they had left Italy and settled in a corner of France where the summers were equally warm. The painter and the plasterer were of Spanish extraction, born in France of parents who crossed the Pyrenees to get away from the Spanish Civil War. The carpenter and the electrician were the kind of Gascons for whom France is essentially another country, somewhere north of the Dordogne. The cosmopolitan character of the area is added to by the many North African Arabs who live here, having chosen to follow their French employers when they left Algeria. It is a curious thing that, just as in Welsh villages men get names from what they do, like Dai the Post or Evans the Milk, some of these Arabs are named in the same way. There's Mohammed Yellow, also known as Mohammed the Spray, because he drives a tractor through the orchards pulling a machine which billows out huge clouds of yellow fog. It treats the trees against disease, but it also permeates everywhere, in the lungs, the clothes, the skin of the operator. Many of the farmers hate this work, and call in Mohammed Yellow to do it for them. Another well-known local Arab is called Ali Poubelle – Ali Dustbin – because he makes a living searching through the public dustbins and rubbish heaps. However, there were no Arabs in the Pigeon-House Gang.

So there they were, cosmopolitan and colourful, on one side, and there we were on the other, a reserved Englishman, the first they had ever worked for, with a charming and volatile French wife. I couldn't speak their French and had not yet the manners to shake hands on sight or to wish them 'bon appetit' every time they went home to lunch or dinner. They were used to dealing with clients who quibbled over every franc, and they were at first surprised and then delighted at our 'OK, get on with it' attitude. There was a certain awkwardness to begin with. Like many men in the south-west, they were inclined to consider women second-class citizens but they were obliged to take their instructions from Marie-Anne because they understood her. However, Marie-Anne's convent education, though strong on social behaviour and how to run a household, was noticeably weak on technical and building terms. I knew most of the English words but could not translate them into French. There were times when they had to wait while I went into the house to consult a dictionary, and came back and told Marie-Anne, who told them. But gradually we got to know them, and they, particularly the employers, who knew what they were charging us, were very pleasant towards us.

M. Torello, the employer of the masons, was of Sicilian extraction, a man of medium height, thick set, with black hair slicked back from a very high forehead, black eyes, and a quiet voice like a crow with laryngitis. He would have made a convincing Godfather with no make-up at all. His gentle manner belied the fact that he was the trainer of the local karate team, and local gossip had it that he was a bit of a goer at the old time dancing club. He did not work himself, beyond touring the various sites he had in progress, saying a few words to his men and reassuring the clients.

The most important of M. Torello's men were Pierre and Jean, who were identical twins. Unlike almost all the other French workmen we came to know, they worked in silence, speaking only when they were spoken to, and then were perfectly relaxed and polite. They usually worked as a pair, and I often watched them, fascinated by their skill and speed, and became convinced that they were genuinely telepathic. Each seemed to know exactly what

the other wanted and when, and would hand it to him, without a word being exchanged. They had the doors off Mme Rambaud's north-light arch and the hole filled in no time. They removed the rabbit hutches from the south wall and then opened an identical arch in it, and made good the sides and the curved top with brickwork of a neatness and precision fit to win prizes, and there was the living room with a view to the south over the fields and orchards.

The chain-link fencing and posts having been removed from the aviary, it was obvious that the space would make a natural terrace in front of what would be the kitchen and the living room. We ourselves wanted a new bathroom in the main house and there was space, we thought, to make this extension towards the pigeonnier and still leave a roomy terrace. 'No problem,' said M. Torello, like the Godfather about to arrange a concrete suit for an irritating rival, 'the boys will put you a bathroom there.'

We had arrived at the end of March. It was now mid-June and the weather began to get very hot, the temperature soaring into the nineties. But nothing slowed up Pierre and Jean. Sustained by quantities of figs from the old tree at the opposite end of the terrace, and aided by a carpenter, who put on the roof, they conjured up the bathroom extension in less than two weeks. Then they had to knock a doorway through the outside wall of our house, built of stone and three feet thick, from the bedroom into the new bathroom. The doorway took the place of one of the huge floor-to-ceiling cupboards, half of which the carpenters fitted into the corner of the new bathroom as a linen cupboard. The other half is still somewhere in the barn.

Next on the scene were the plumbers. M. de Cany, who employed them, was a rather aloof character whose main concern seemed to be to create the impression that if, despite his noble name, he was in trade and the plumbing trade at that, it was all due to some unfortunate chain of circumstance which he pre-ferred not to detail. He was as distant with us as he was with M. Torello and the other employers. His visits were always short. He would have a few words with M. Bellin, if he was there, give his instructions briefly to his men, and leave. His workmen, the wraith-like M. Bienvenue in his antique overalls and cap and a large, fat, good-natured youth who was 'learning the trade', looked like a music-hall comedy act. It was clear that M. Bienvenue had nothing whatever left to learn about plumbing. Once or twice I pointed out that M. de Cany had suggested doing something in a particular way. His replies to these comments tended to be 'Really?' or 'Dare say he did' or even a scornful 'Hah!', while he continued to follow his own path. He may always have been like that, or he may have been indulging himself, as he was, I discovered, only two months from retirement.

Auguste, the fat boy, was willing but not particularly able. His chief interest was birds and one day something happened which excited him a good deal more than plumbing. As I passed the barn one morning I noticed a patch of white on the ground, like a new tennis ball or a large piece of cotton wool. When I looked closer, I saw that it was a baby barn owl.

At some time in the past someone had fixed a long, narrow wooden box with four openings like those in dove-cotes, high on the wall of the barn under the roof of the auvent. I knew it was occupied by a pair of barn owls, and the baby had clearly fallen from or been kicked out of the family home. It was alive, though in a state of shock. I had no idea what to do with it. I went round and mentioned it to the masons, who were putting roughcast on the newly finished bathroom.

'I've just found a baby barn owl,' I said. Their reaction to this announcement was about the same as if I had said, 'I've just seen a blade of grass': non-existent. I went into the lean-to, where Auguste and M. Bienvenue were turning the back third into a modern bathroom, and tried again.

'I've just found a baby barn owl,' I said.

M. Bienvenue ignored me and carried on turning his piece of pipe. At the time I did not know but I have found out during several years' acquaintance with French countrymen that their interest in and knowledge of bird and animal life is strictly confined to creatures which are edible. There are exceptions to this basic rule, and Auguste was one of them.

'Where? Where?' he said, excited.

'By the barn,' I said, reasonably enough. 'I'll show you.'

The baby barn owl was motionless, but clearly alive and

apparently unhurt. 'It was probably pushed out of the nest,' said Auguste. 'I've heard that often one of the parents turns against the young, and they have to be protected by the other, or they get eaten. I've got several birds. I could look after it.'

Well, I found a cardboard box, made some holes in the sides and the lid, put some straw in the bottom, and the baby owl on the straw, and Auguste took it home strapped to the back of his bicycle. Sadly, he turned out to be less successful as an owl-mother than as a plumber. He reported a week later that the bird had died. We still have the barn owls, and there is a similar incident almost every year. Early this summer I found two of the young on the ground beneath the nesting box, both dead.

M. Loubradou, the carpenter, differed from the others in that he was a genuine entrepreneur rather than an artisan. He employed fifteen men, and had a big business restoring châteaux, churches and country houses, and manufacturing garden sheds and Scandinavian-type wooden holiday homes. He was a Gascon whose French was, according to Marie-Anne, who had now got to grips with the local version, perfectly correct, though spoken with an accent you could have cut in slices. He and the electrician, M. Galan, held long conversations in the local language, Occitan. This is the old language, not a dialect, of the south of France, the Langue d'Oc. In earlier times France was divided more or less across the middle by an irregular and imaginary line north of which the people spoke the Langue d'Oi, in which the word for 'yes' was 'oui', and south of which they spoke the Langue d'Oc, in which 'yes' was 'oc'. Though the French of the north became the official language long ago, the language of the south has never died, and still thrives today. It has its poets and writers, classes for children on local radio and in some schools, societies, and even a movement for the establishment of an independent Occitania. You will often see cars in the south-west with the letters 'OC' on the back, to show that the driver believes in Occitania. At present the movement is far more cultural than political or economic.

M. Loubradou had an ashen complexion, stooped, and his head and hands trembled slightly. When I first met him, I wondered whether he would be able to see the job through. But I need not have worried. I met him again several years later, and learned that he had had to take on more men to cope with the expansion of his business and had also become the mayor of his village. His head and hands still trembled, he was as pale as ever, but clearly there was nothing wrong with him except that he shook a bit. He was one of those rare and encouraging men who never back away from a problem. As soon as it was posed, he started thinking positively about how it could best be solved.

There was a good one for him in the pigeonnier. We planned to put the bedroom upstairs, as I said, but there was a problem with the roof. From a height of about six feet at the side walls the tiled roof soared steeply upwards and inwards on all four sides for another twelve feet or so. As a general rule in this part of France, the roof consists of bare tiles resting on battens, with no close-boarding or other form of insulation on the inside. This is the case with almost all farms and old houses, and with many new ones as well. It is an economical system but has the disadvantage that as the tiles become old and weather-worn, they leak. A further disadvantage is that in winter the space immediately beneath the roof becomes extremely cold, and in summer unbearably hot. Traditionally this was of no consequence because the space was normally used for storing bales of hay, an unbeatable insulation, as birds, mice and dormice well appreciated, or for other storage. I had realised that the summer temperatures would make the room extremely uncomfortable for sleeping, and that the answer was insulation. But was it possible? The roof was supported by a splendid system of main beams, secondary beams, cross members, and rafters, perhaps more intricate than was structurally necessary in order to provide a maximum of perching space for the pigeons. How would it be possible to get the insulation, whatever it might be, between this forest of woodwork, and more important, hold it in position?

I asked Marie-Anne to put the problem to M. Loubradou. He stared upwards in silence, shaking slightly and rotating slowly.

'Not easy,' he said. 'Not easy at all. But it can be done.'

He proposed to put up a ceiling of plaster panels with a four-inch thickness of fibreglass insulation behind them. As the roof had been built some two hundred years earlier, before the existence of mechanical saws, the oak beams had been cut from the tree and were very roughly finished by hand. No one of them was quite straight, some curved slightly in opposite directions, no two were parallel, and there seemed no way in which flat, straight plaster panels could be matched with the countless inequalities. But, in principle, the answer was simple. It consisted in fixing a very light aluminium rod framework to the rafters, into which the plaster panels fitted neatly. The aluminium rods were all parallel with each other, and the only thing that varied was the length of the little brackets which fixed them to the beams, the shortest where the beam came furthest into the room space, the others following the conformation of each beam.

It was a job that required scaffolding, so the new floor had to be put in first to support the weight. This was done by taking the old one and all its joists away, and replacing them with strong pine rafters on which a floor of 22mm hardboard was fixed. So the living room acquired a beamed ceiling, and the bedroom a new floor. The insulation was done last of all, and left some of the main beams exposed, so that aesthetically as well as practically it was a great success.

There was still two centuries of dust visible on the beams apart from the residue of decades of pigeon droppings and I asked M. Loubradou to leave his scaffolding for a few days so that I could clean, treat and varnish them. The two main oak beams, which crossed the room parallel with the floor, and which carried the weight of all those above, appeared to my inexperienced eye to be completely rotten. In places I could pinch them to dust between my fingers, but M. Loubradou assured me that that was of no importance – the heart was good, he said. But I didn't like the look of them, so I started to knock off the rotten bits. Once started I had to finish, and I ended with a floor covered in wood dust and splinters, and beams not much more than half the diameter they had been. But M. Loubradou was right, the inside was as hard as iron, and I learned at first hand what 'heart of oak' really means.

Gradually the pigeonnier was transformed. We took away Mme Rambaud's ladder and replaced it by a plain pine staircase. We had wooden shutters fitted to the doors and windows, in keeping with the usual custom in this part of France. They not only add a certain charm to the exterior, but are also a good security measure, and help to insulate the houses against extremes of temperature.

Mme Rambaud's studio became a living room sixteen feet square with large French doors giving a view across orchards and fields and opening on to a gravel terrace which forms another living room for outdoor meals, lounging and sunbathing. The former chicken-house became a spacious kitchen/breakfast room, plus a modern bathroom, reached somewhat informally by a door from the kitchen. Well, it was the most logical use of the space, and nobody has ever complained. Upstairs, there is just the bedroom, with its beams and a window which lets in the morning sun.

Eventually the work was completed and the gang folded their tool kits and silently stole away, well satisfied with their loot.

Borne down by the burden of social security payments for his men, and realising no doubt that he would never strike such a little gold mine again, M. Torello retired to dance a sinister Sicilian swathe through the perfumed widows of the south.

M. Loubradou trembled from strength to strength and was recently restoring the nearby Château de Lauzun, originally the seventeenth-century home of the notorious Duc de Lauzun, courtier to Louis XIV. While the king dallied with his mistress, Madame de Montespan, Lauzan, who thought of her as his protectress, would hide under the bed to check on whether she spoke of him as well as she said she did. Today the château is the property of a gentleman who made a fortune from a hypermarket franchise in Bordeaux.

M. de Cany has opened a shop for bathroom fittings, full of gilded mirrors, pastel-coloured baths, goldy taps, pretty tiles and complicated shower arrangements. M. Bellin and M. Morgan have both recently retired, M. Bellin to a new resort development on the Mediterranean coast. Perhaps occasionally, over a bottle of Bordeaux or two, they stare dreamily out to sea and revive hazy memories of the pigeon-house coup.

Did they all swindle us? Perhaps, but I remember the gang with something like affection, because, in their enthusiasm, they left behind an old house into which new life had been breathed, and a gem of a cottage which has proved as full of life and happiness as Aladdin's cave was full of jewels.

Chapter Five

What's the Weather Like?

This is what we asked everybody, when we first thought of moving to south-west France, and it is what everybody asks us. I remember on our first exploratory visit asking a petrol station attendant if it snowed in winter. He looked at me in astonishment and after a pause said, 'Well, it did snow here about ten years ago, and it stayed on the ground for nearly an hour.' When I asked that question it was 1982, and 1985, of which more later, was still to come.

Very few of the local population have ever been to England, but they are all convinced that the climate is wet and cold and, especially in London, permanently foggy, and it would not be hard to persuade some of them that we still have gas lamps and hansom cabs. It is no use telling them that much of northern France is colder and wetter than London, and that since the passing of the Clean Air Act banning coal fires there have been no real fogs in London. Their idea of London seems to be taken from some early Sherlock Holmes film in black and white, and nothing will change it.

M. Rambaud was soon telling us how pleased we would be to get away from the London weather. The micro-climate is a popular conception in France, as M. Rambaud was well aware, and he thought we would like one. 'Here, beside the river, we have our own micro-climate,' he said. 'It is warmer here than for miles around. Storms pass us by. It can be raining hard in town, and not a drop here,' and so on. We listened. We could see the rich vegetation, the mimosas, the yuccas, the palm trees, and were not really seeking to be reassured.

I had spent most of my life in southern England where you

never knew what the weather would do next, except that it was not likely to be that marvellous, and the nearest it could get to a fog was an occasional sea mist. I had also spent some time in equatorial Africa, where every day is the same length all year round, it is always too hot, and the rainy seasons are a good deal more punctual than British Rail. We soon found that the climate of south-west France lies well between the two and is hard to beat for sheer liveability, though the so-called micro-climate was, of course, another of M. Rambaud's fantasies.

Most of the rain we get falls in the first four months of the year. But there are also lots of sunny days, and the winter is virtually over by mid-February. By then the first of the daffodils are in flower around the old lime tree behind the house, and that is the signal for Marie-Anne, who loves flowers, to start filling stone containers and big red terracotta pots with yellow or purple pansies, and brilliantly coloured primulas. It might be thought that with ten acres of land it would be easy to find somewhere to put flowers, but it is always a problem. The orchards come close to the house, the garden around the swimming pool has to be almost entirely lawns, and the garden in front of the house includes gravel areas for access to the barn and the house, and a lawn around a lily pond. So we have solved the problem by concentrating on flowering shrubs and trees, and flowers in pots all over the place. Geraniums on the terraces, huge pots of petunias on the edges of the swimming pool, begonias and busy lizzies on the north side of the house, silk trees, catalpas, bananas, tree hibiscus, Indian lilacs and tamarisk here and there on the pool lawns. There are arum lilies and cannas by the barn, a few rambling roses, rhododendrons in a shady corner, but the only flowerbed is in front of the 'chauffeur's room' facing south, and we fill it with dahlias, which like it there and grow up to six feet tall carrying hundreds of flowers through the summer.

There were a few summer days in our childhood that were so hot that my sister and I were allowed to put the lawn sprinklers on and run in and out of the spray to keep cool – private swimming pools were almost unheard of then. They were isolated occasions, years apart. Here, temperatures in the eighties and nineties arrive in June and continue almost uninterrupted through

July and August and into September. Every summer since we came here has been long, sunny and hot, often lasting through October. There may be an occasional grey day, a storm and a tropical downpour, but the sun soon returns.

Autumns tend to be serene and golden. Winters are usually mild, but there are sometimes cold spells. Spring is the rainy season, creating a reserve of water in the fertile soil which helps to produce the wonderful variety of fruit and vegetables which thrive here. April can be hot and sunny enough to use the pool, or cool grey and showery. So, in general, there are clear-cut seasons and the weather is benevolent, and fairly predictable. Ah, but in particular, it can do some unusual, and very violent things.

Take, for example, our first 23rd June, which was a Saturday. The workmen, with the exception of M. Bienvenue, who kept his cap and overalls on through everything, had been stripped to the waist and in shorts for two or three weeks while the thermometer climbed to the high nineties and stuck there. On Friday night, not long after they had gone home for the weekend – only artisans working on their own account would dream of working on a Saturday and then only when really pressed – the sky turned a strange, dirty copper colour, and everything became very still. We waited up, expecting a storm. Nothing happened. We went to bed just before midnight to the sound of distant thunder. As the minutes passed lightning played on the clouds and the thunder rolled nearer, then suddenly there was a sizzling flash that lit up the whole sky and silhouetted the trees, followed immediately by a titanic, earth-shaking crash of thunder.

The performance which followed was awe-inspiring in its violence, like nothing I had ever experienced in England. The thunder was louder, the lightning more vicious, and the rain was so impressive that we switched on the porch light so that we could see it falling. We stared at it, fascinated. It was like standing in a cave entrance behind a waterfall. I had seen something like it only once before, in equatorial Africa. A Sicilian count who represented one of the international economic aid projects in the Third World had driven me a hundred miles in his high-powered Mercedes to look at a model village which thirty years before had been built deep in the jungle by Marie-Anne's father to house the employees of his sawmill. I had been impressed, not to say terrified, by his driving technique on the way there. On the red earth African road, he ignored potholes, bumps and other obstacles of various kinds and maintained his speed at about 60 m.p.h. no matter what. He hit and presumably killed one pig and two chickens, and might well have had a couple of Africans if they had been slower on their feet. That was on the way there. On the way back we ran into the mother and father of all African rainstorms; the water fell in an impenetrable sheet and the road became a river, marked only by the trees on either side. It was impossible to see ahead. The car, however, continued at the same speed through the wall of water with the mad Sicilian count smiling happily to himself. He glanced at me once, saying, 'I drive in ze Safari Rally. Is a good practice.' It lasted twenty minutes and then became an everyday African downpour.

I had told Marie-Anne, no doubt too often, of this experience, and was about to turn to her to say, 'Now you can really see what it was like that time in Africa,' when I heard her say, 'Oh, my God!'

In brief, the rain was falling inside the house as well as outside. A small waterfall was plopping gently down the side of the staircase and sending a stream slowly across the tiles of the hall. Upstairs there was the best part of an inch of water on the landing carpet and drips were falling in various places in the other rooms. In the middle of the night it was a case for buckets and towels – there was nothing else to be done.

'There are buckets in the kitchen under the sink,' said Marie-Anne. She was right, and there was also a flood all over the kitchen floor, considerably worse than anything upstairs. As I mentioned earlier, the kitchen was a side extension to the house, converted from the former pigsty, and with nothing above it but its own roof, apparently porous, and probably untouched since the days of the pigs.

We put all the buckets and bowls we could find under the worst of the drips, then towels and mats to block the doorways and prevent the flood spreading from the kitchen and the bathroom. By the time we had done all this the rain outside was becoming less torrential, and we thought we could detect an easing off of the internal drips. We went to bed in the downstairs bedroom, where there were only a couple of steady drips. Marie-Anne, not the tearful kind but close to tears, contented herself with a short and pithy description of M. Rambaud's parentage, and then we lay silent, listening to the drips, and finally went to sleep. Dripped off is the appropriate term.

Before coming to this house I had had nothing to do with 'do-it-yourself' activities. I may have dabbed a bit of paint here or there, but had never tried anything more ambitious. In my schooldays I had been taught woodwork, but always bodged everything to the point where I dared not even take it home to show my indulgent mother. The woodwork master, a Captain Flood, a one-legged veteran of World War I, was in the habit of emphasising my clumsiness by tapping me on the head with a wooden mallet: 'You call that a (bang) mortice and (bang) tenon, boy? You'll have to try again (bang), won't you, boy?' As a result of this treatment I had steered clear of hammers and chisels ever since. But needs must when the devil drives.

Saturday morning was warm and sunny. The storm had cleared the air. There was still water everywhere in the house, though the dripping had stopped. But it was clear that something had to be done about the roof. It was equally clear that it would be impossible to get a workman to do it. No Gascon workman would dream of working on a Saturday or Sunday. Saturday, just possibly in an emergency. But to the average Gascon a leaky roof is as much an emergency as a duck getting its feet wet. If anything was to be done at once, I would have to do it.

When we had done most of the mopping up, and Marie-Anne was busy pegging up mats and towels to dry in the sun, I said I was going to have a look at the kitchen roof. Knowing my previous form, she made a sound which might well have been a snort of derision.

I fetched a ladder from the barn and climbed up and peered over the gutter. There was an area about eight feet square in which all the tiles were flaky and a few actually had holes in, and fell apart as I took them off.

I had noticed in the barn, without paying much attention, that there were two stacks of old tiles. I had assumed that as

M. Rambaud had left them, they must be useless, but I searched through them and found about a hundred of the same pattern as those on the kitchen roof. It was just about enough. It was not until I started to take the bad tiles off and had thrown them down from the ladder that I saw that the battens on which they had to be hooked were completely rotted away in parts and would have to be replaced. Enough remained for me to see how the roof was done, and to copy the system. I had to make a quick trip to the local builders' merchant, fortunately open on Saturday mornings, to buy enough for the job.

So I set about it, measuring, sawing, hammering, hooking the tiles on and sliding them under each other. This was a problem at first. Some seemed harder to fit than others, until I realised that they only went one way round, and I was trying to put them on upside down. It was extremely hot on the roof, and as the day wore on it became hotter and hotter. I became possessed with a mad determination to get the job done. I refused to stop for lunch, and worked on, filthy and soaked to the skin in sweat. It was after six o'clock when I put the last tile in place and crawled shakily down the ladder, exhausted and dizzy from the heat.

A cold beer, a hot bath and a good dinner began the process of restoration. In the heat of the day the house had dried out, the buckets were put away, the mats and towels dried and put back in their proper place. After the meal I took a stroll outside, aching all over but feeling virtuous. The sun was no longer shining, the sky I noticed at once had gone that eerie copper colour, shading to purple. I saw a flicker of lightning, and then heard a distant rumble. The next one was louder and closer.

I went back indoors. 'It's buckets and towels again,' I said. 'There is going to be another storm.' Within half an hour, much earlier than the previous night, we were enjoying another spectacular performance. At first there were just the great thunder crashes, shaking the house, and the lightning sizzling through the trees, then suddenly the flood gates opened and down came the rain. Within a few minutes the roof was leaking again, but we had placed the buckets and towels in the strategic spots, and the damage was limited. When the leaks had started upstairs, I had gone straight to the kitchen and stood there staring at the ceiling.

Marie-Anne had shown her lack of confidence in my day's labour, or perhaps just her prudence, by placing buckets in what had been the worst places. I waited. Not a drop. Not a single drop. Nothing. After a decent interval, I took the two buckets upstairs as reinforcements.

'We don't need these down there,' I said, casually. 'There's no water coming in.'

Marie-Anne stared. 'I don't believe it,' she said, heading downstairs to the kitchen.

'Well,' she said.

'Well what?'

She smiled. 'Well done.'

The rain was still pouring down, and still not a drop inside the kitchen. I was finding it hard to believe. I had never in my life done anything like it. I seemed to hear the ghost of Captain Flood saying, 'Got it right for once, did you, boy?' The world is, of course, full of handymen who would have made nothing of this job, but to me, who had spent half a lifetime sitting at a desk in various newspaper offices bashing a typewriter, it seemed a considerable achievement, and if I have lingered rather over this incident of the roof, it is because in a way it made me a different person. In thirty years, Marie-Anne, amiably enough, had never considered writing to be real work. Farmers, doctors, carpenters, garage mechanics and people like that worked. Writers wrote. But fixing the roof gave me the confidence to tackle all kinds of maintenance and repair jobs which in the past I, and everybody who knew me, would have considered completely beyond my capabilities. With so much to do around the place we were lucky that it happened so soon after we came here. Not having to call a workman for every little job has saved us a good deal of money.

We have had other violent summer storms but none quite as bad as that. In most summers there are some storms, but there have also been summers with none at all. But when the weather here occasionally drops its cloak of benevolence, it can play some nasty tricks, and we have been subjected to other forms of nuisance and violence, tree-flattening gales, hail stones as big as golf balls, and dust storms and drought among them. But the disasters are short-lived and add just enough excitement and variety to avoid the boredom that must come with a climate that is always good and completely predictable.

Chapter Six

FRIENDS AND NEIGHBOURS

Everybody who moves from one house to another wonders what their new neighbours will be like. Like mothers-in-law, troublesome neighbours are always good for a laugh, so long as they are other people's, not your own.

We were very lucky. Though utterly unlike each other both M. Caumont and M. Lambert and their families have been far nicer to us than we had any right to expect. Towards each other, however, they showed little warmth.

They were both Gascons, born and bred, descendants of generations of peasant farmers. They were the same age and had known each other all their lives, and had been at the village school together. M. Caumont had become more a modern farmer than a peasant, having taken a degree in agronomy as a young man. He specialised in fruit farming, plums, apples and pears, and some cereals. He is solidly built, blue-eyed, fairly tall, with a calm, good-natured manner, coupled with shrewdness and the quiet confidence of a man who knows his trade from top to bottom. His orchards are always neat, his farm buildings spick and span, his tractors and other equipment in working order. Before finalising the purchase of our house we had made an agreement with M. Caumont for him to look after our orchards, which in a good year produce between twenty and thirty tons of plums. He does all the work, and so takes the lion's share of any net profits, which in lean years are non-existent. He has steadily improved the orchards, and has done it with great efficiency, and with scrupulous honesty.

M. Lambert's method of farming was completely different. He was a subsistence farmer in the old tradition, whose creed was 'If you produce it yourself, you'll never have to buy it.' He had a plum orchard, but also grew maize. He kept some cows, and bred calves for veal. He had free-range chickens, ducks, geese, pigeons and guinea-fowl. He had apple trees and a vineyard, a row of beehives and a group of walnut trees. His farm is approached down a long drive lined with fruit trees and vines, and the entrance to the farmyard is flanked by two fine horse-chestnut trees. His old mother told me that she had planted the trees herself from chestnuts which he brought home from school one day more than fifty years ago.

The buildings around M. Lambert's farmyard have a medieval appearance, without actually being ruins, and look as if they have hardly been touched for a hundred years. Without much trouble you can imagine a young D'Artagnan mounting a rather seedy nag and flourishing off to seek fame and fortune from just such a setting. The yard would have been dirt and mud then and is now tarmacadam but that is the only wrong note.

M. Lambert's concession to modernity was to use tractors instead of horses. He had three of them, all ancient, including a David Brown which he told me he had bought in the 1950s after much opposition from his father. It is still in working order.

Unlike M. Caumont, who had a grown-up son to help him, M. and Mme Lambert did all the work on the farm themselves, with occasional help from their schoolgirl daughter, who could already drive a tractor. Physically, M. Lambert was small and wiry, with a sallow complexion and lank brown hair. He stooped rather, and had a strange, furtive manner, speaking out of the side of his mouth and always looking somewhere else. In some ways he reminded me of an old lag whose life story I once wrote for a magazine, who had spent almost all his adult life, more than thirty years, in repeated spells in prison for incorrigible thieving. But M. Lambert was, in fact, a kind and completely honest man whose father had been mayor of the local village and his uncle the village priest. His oddness was due entirely to excessive timidity. Neither he nor M. Caumont were typical Gascons; the false bonhomie, the braggadocio, the easy-come, easy-go deviousness not known in these parts, were completely foreign to their natures. Each in his own way was a serious man. M. Caumont was at ease in company, went to meetings and conferences as far afield as

California, and made speeches on behalf of French fruitgrowers' co-operatives. M. Lambert went nowhere. He was a loner, and continued to farm in his own way, as his father had farmed half a century before.

While every other grower for miles around had joined the local co-operative where, to make them into prunes, the plums are dried on belts which move slowly through tunnels where very hot air blows over them continuously, M. Lambert dried his own plums in a decrepit prune oven. For many years this was heated by a fire of logs of oak, hornbeam and fruit wood, but eventually, about fifteen years ago, M. Lambert had changed to heating with an oil-fired burner. The plums were stacked in trays on metal trolleys which were pushed into the oven along metal rails. The plums were left in the oven for about four hours to make the delicious prunes called 'mi-cuit' (half-dried), or all night to produce the normal, dryer prune.

Prunes were 'invented' in the early Middle Ages when some greedy monk strolling through a plum orchard took a bite at a plum which had lain on the ground for weeks in the sun and become black and shrivelled. He was surprised to find that it tasted delicious. For hundreds of years after this prunes were produced by placing ripe plums on slatted trays shaped rather like snow-shoes, and leaving them in the full sun to dry. These trays are still made and sold to tourists as souvenirs.

The majority of British visitors to this part of France have at first little sympathy for the prune. When I first came here my attitude was the same. It comes from having been told as children that 'prunes are good for you', and from all those disgusting school lunches which concluded with a plate containing two or three black objects looking like long-dead mice in a pool of runny custard. When a visiting English rugby team came to play a 'friendly' with the team from Agen, who are often champions of France, prunes were served as dessert at the lunch of honour. It led to a lot of caustic and ribald comment and a certain amount of scornful hilarity among the English players, including suggestions that it was a not very subtle attempt at sabotage. Some of the Agen players were fruit farmers, and all were proud of the fact that Agen is 'the capital of prunes' as well as of rugby. Fortunately the

Gascons were not great linguists and did not understand much of what was said. Even so, umbrage was taken, and the teams are said nearly to have come to blows before the match.

Such are the effects of prejudice and misunderstanding. To compare a school dinner prune of revolting memory with the real thing, sweet, succulent, delicately perfumed, is to equate Algerian plonk with vintage Bordeaux wine, or lumpfish roe with Beluga caviar. Those of our visitors who have tasted the prunes from our own orchard, bottled in Armagnac brandy by Marie-Anne, become unanimously enthusiastic, and go and buy their own supply in the local shops. It took me some time to find out why they always said to Marie-Anne, 'They are very good, but not as good as yours.' Some people soak the prunes overnight in cold tea or an infusion of lime flowers before bottling them and some add sugar syrup, but the usual method is to put the prunes in a solution of equal parts of distilled water and Armagnac brandy and seal them in an airtight jar. After a few weeks, the longer the better, the prunes absorb some of the liquid, and the level falls. The jars are then opened and topped up with more of the same solution, and resealed until required. Marie-Anne's praise-winning variation turned out to be that she tops up with pure Armagnac.

Despite his 'antiquated' methods, M. Lambert's prunes were if anything better than the co-operative version, which are dried slightly harder to withstand packing and transport all over Europe. Best of all are his 'mi-cuit', which are too juicy to transport commercially. These are delicious on their own, but after being bottled in Armagnac they make a splendid dessert when served with some of their own juice and the ice-cream called 'Vanilla des Iles'.

M. Lambert also made his own wine which, though rather less successful than his prunes, could in good years be described by connoisseurs in a generous mood as 'drinkable'. At three francs a litre, he had a regular clientele of well-pickled drinkers who found it more than acceptable in any year. It was, with eggs, potatoes and pigeons, one of the few things he sold to the public, that is, to anyone who happened to ask.

Only a few years ago every farmer in this part of France had his own private vineyard, producing wine for his own and the family's consumption. This is less usual than it was but there are still a great many of them. Vines are, as a rule, easy to grow and very productive. It does not need much land to produce enough wine for a year for one family, and it is quite common to see small modern bungalows with a vineyard about the size of a normal vegetable plot taking up part of the garden.

Harvesting grapes in the traditional manner is hard work, labour intensive, and not a job that can ever be done single-handed. Many of the big Bordeaux vineyards, though few of the great wines, now harvest with machines whose tall wheels pass either side of the vine row with the driver perched high above. In M. Lambert's vineyard the harvesting machinery consisted of scissors and buckets, and the grape harvest was an occasion when family and friends all joined in.

When the time came at the end of our first summer, I thought it would be neighbourly to offer to lend a hand. I have since become 'our Englishman' to the locals but at that time I was still regarded with circumspection, like some unfamiliar animal, probably harmless, but better to be wary of. My offer was met with courteous surprise, and M. Lambert felt it his duty to warn me. 'It's hard work, and it's going to be very hot today.' I assured him that I would join them as soon as I had done one or two errands for Marie-Anne.

It was a commonly held belief among the local farmers that M. Lambert's vines were illegal, because they belonged to a variety subject to attack by the phylloxera bug which from 1864 onwards for thirty years destroyed the vineyards throughout France. Whether it was true or not is another matter. It might just have been their way of underlining M. Lambert's attachment to the past. But it is also possible that, while the commercial wine producers followed the general line and uprooted their vineyards and replanted with resistant stock from America, some farmers in out-of-the-way places may just have shrugged their shoulders and carried on. Whatever the variety of grapes, M. Lambert's three acres of vines would not have won any medals for neatness; some of the wires on which they were trained were rusted and broken and there was a healthy crop of weeds between the rows. On the other hand the vines were heavy with purple fruit.

At about ten o'clock I joined a dozen other pickers, who had already been at work for a couple of hours. It was a crew fairly described as motley, with a couple of schoolchildren taking a day off, an old lady in the peasant black, various cousins and brothers, and two robust and ribald peasant women, all in a museum collection of straw hats as protection against the sun. My own straw boater from my sons' well-known school was much commented upon, if not admired. I was given a blue bucket and a pair of scissors and assigned a row opposite one of the cousins or brothers. Whoever he was, he knew what he was about. When the buckets were full they had to be emptied into a sort of hopper at the side of the field. Before I had filled my first bucket, he had already emptied three.

I soon found that in addition to the big fat bunches of grapes, there were also malformed bunches with shrivelled or unformed grapes, and only two or three good ones. As M. Lambert passed me with a full bucket, I asked him what to do about them. He muttered a reply, hardly pausing, from which I understood that if it had a grape on it, it was good. I looked to see what those nearest me were doing. Nothing was wasted, everything went in including bits of twig and an occasional leaf.

I became a little more adept with practice but soon everyone, including the old lady, had passed me, going in the other direction down a different row. When I started my second row, I found myself opposite one of the jovial wenches, who slowed up to talk to me, saying among other things that she had never spoken to an 'unglais' before, and that my 'axun' was difficult to understand. Her own accent was as far from school French as Chinese, so our conversation was rather laboured, and as far as she was concerned, hilarious. As the morning became steadily hotter, I was getting even slower and I was pleased to hear the twelve o'clock siren.

There are a few towns in southern France, and our local town is one of them, which sound a siren every day, Sundays included, at midday. It can be heard for miles around, and is the signal for everybody, especially all those workers in the fields, and all the artisans working in the villages and on isolated private houses, to down tools and go to lunch. Everything shuts down except the food shops, which remain open for a further half an hour so that

people can buy something for lunch, if they want. The midday meal is much the most important one in this part of France, and virtually everybody takes the full two hours.

Mme Lambert had already done me the honour of insisting that I should join them for the harvest lunch. It had been decided that it was too hot to eat outside, so it was not one of those bench and trestle table meals so often illustrated in guide books. We ate instead, fourteen of us, at a big table in the cool of the farmhouse kitchen. First, we had a drink all round, a glass of Mme Lambert's home-made walnut aperitif, and some rough and ready introductions were made. My jolly companion was introduced as the wife of Mme Lambert's brother. This proved to be not quite the case, as I learned some months later that she was in fact his concubine, and that his real wife fulfilled this role for one of the cousins.

M. Lambert placed me on his right, and surprised me by muttering a Latin grace as his wife placed a huge tureen of soup in front of him. Perhaps it was the influence of his uncle, the priest. Soup is very popular in this part of France, and practically every meal starts with it, one of its advantages being that it enables a few glasses of wine to be drunk without ill effects, so that work can be readily taken up after lunch. But it is a mistake to think that because there are unlimited supplies of cheap wine available all Frenchmen drink it. There is some alcoholism, though less than in northern France, but a lot of men, and more women, drink very little wine or none at all. M. Lambert had provided plenty of his own wine to go with the meal, but he drank water. The meal continued in typical Gascon fashion with 'confit de canard', for which the region is famous, and which consists of joints of roasted duck which have been bottled in their own refined fat and kept in store for future use. Properly made the confit keeps for at least six months, and joints are removed when required and reheated for meals. Traditionally they are reheated in the oven, surrounded by sliced potatoes which absorb the melting fat and cook in it, and this is how Mme Lambert served it.

The company became quite animated as more wine was drunk, but the moment I tried to say something, all conversation stopped in mid-sentence and everyone stared at me, waiting. For a moment I was non-plussed, and then I recalled a similar occasion from many years before. My sister had married the son of a Lebanese ship-owner and had gone to live in Lebanon. Several years later, when her twin sons were just reaching school age, I visited her for the first time since the marriage. Her husband's family were rich and influential, his older brother was mayor of the town. They were also numerous. Without delay I was invited to the local hotel for lunch, and on arrival found that a banqueting room had been reserved and something like thirty members of the family had foregathered. I was seated in a place of honour next to my brother-in-law's father, and the meal started – in silence. It continued in complete silence, which I began to feel was uneasy. After what seemed an age, my brother-in-law smiled at me across the table and said quietly, 'They are waiting for you to make a speech.' Coming from a country in which speeches normally come after meals, I had simply not thought of this.

'Just say something flattering,' my sister suggested.

My speech was probably quite incoherent, but I included something about how happy I was to be part of such a distinguished family gathering, how beautiful their country was – quite true then, before all the troubles had started – and that I had been surprised by the degree of modernity to be seen everywhere and the sophistication of the people. Since only a few of those present spoke English, my brother-in-law, who had been educated in England, translated. His translation was no doubt a lot smoother than my speech, and went down well; many smiles were directed at me and the silence was transformed into Arabic hubbub.

At M. Lambert's all this came back to me as I started to reply to his tentative inquiry as to what had made me come to Lot-et-Garonne and silence fell. Say something flattering, I told myself. Nobody present understood English so I stumbled on in my rusty French, saying briefly that my work had taken me all over the world, to more than a hundred countries, and that when the time came I had found it very difficult to think of any one of them that would be better to live in than France, and that we had decided that, all in all, this part of France had more to offer than any other, and how fortunate we had been to find ourselves with such friendly neighbours.

This was well received, though with a touch of embarrassment by M. Lambert, but it did not alter the fact that each time I started to say something, there was immediate silence. This reaction continued until the meal was approaching its end, by which time it seemed that they had accepted me as one of them, and the atmosphere became more normal. Mme Lambert offered a 'crème de noix', a walnut liqueur, from an ancient and anonymous bottle which was passed reverently round the table like vintage port. Both walnut aperitif and walnut liqueurs are made not from the walnuts themselves, as one might suppose, but from the green husks macerated in alcohol. All farmers' wives have their own variations on the method, some adding a few mashed unripe nuts, or different kinds and quantities of sugar.

After lunch they went back to the vines and I, having made my neighbourly gesture, returned home.

On the south side of the Lamberts' house, there is a kitchen garden about fifty metres long and ten metres wide where Mme Lambert grows all her own vegetables, except potatoes which M. Lambert grows in an acre plot beside the river. With shiny purple aubergines, orange and green pimentoes, fat tomatoes, dark green courgettes, marrows and cucumbers, haricot beans and butter beans, radishes, onions, garlic, parsley and several other herbs, Mme Lambert's kitchen garden seemed to have something of everything. It was enough for me to buy a dozen eggs at little more than half the market price for her to add in whatever she had that week, free of charge.

On a typical farm in the south-west the farmer retires at sixty-five and his son takes over. The old parents continue to live on the farm and with the family, and still do odd jobs around the property. Often it is the grandfather, called 'pépé' in the family, who looks after the vineyard, while the 'mémé', the grandmother, helps in the kitchen. The farmer's wife, in addition to running the household and feeding everybody, is expected to take charge of the kitchen garden and the farmyard animals, chickens, ducks and so on.

When we first came here, both old Mme Lambert and old Mme Caumont were still alive, the grandfathers having died some years before. Mère Lambert was over eighty and walked with sticks, bent almost double with arthritis, but often when I went round to the Lamberts in summer for eggs or potatoes, I would find her sitting in the shade beneath the porch, plucking a chicken for the pot, or, with a bowl on her knees and a bucket at her side, paring apples. She had the reputation of having been as hard as nails and savagely mean, but in her old age she had become almost amiable and was always pleased to have a chat. Conversation was not easy as she was rather deaf, but she was shrewd and was a mine of rustic lore about the weather and the crops. She had a habit of reminding me what saint's day it was, and what saying went with it: 'Tout planté avant la Ste Catherine, prend racine' suggests that everything planted before St Catherine's day (25th November) will thrive, while 'A la St Robert, tout arbre est vert' means that by St Robert's day (30th April) all the trees are in leaf. In French almost all these old sayings rhyme.

Mère Lambert died at eighty-four, of nothing in particular, just worn out by old age and a lifetime of hard work. One of M. Lambert's chief problems was that in addition to his own farm, he also worked his old mother's farm, five miles away on the other side of the village, which she had steadfastly refused to part with. He was constantly dashing from one to the other. After his mother's death he continued to work it, though he said he would sell the farmhouse, and he had the roof renovated in readiness for a sale. Unfortunately, he had a surly and solitary tenant who refused to leave. M. Lambert asked him to go but he stayed, and M. Lambert was much too gentle and easy-going to try seriously to turn anyone out.

Then M. Lambert himself became ill. He spent several spells in hospital, returning at regular intervals in between for radiation treatment. Back at home he went on working as usual. Neither he nor his wife ever mentioned the nature of his illness. I never heard him complain. He always replied to the usual 'Comment va?' (How are you?) with 'Ça va, merci' ('All right, thank you'). He struggled on for more than two years. I saw him on his tractor, ploughing away, only two weeks before Mme Lambert told me that he had died in hospital. The whole village turned out for his funeral service. The old Norman church was crammed, and people who could not get in stood on the steps and halfway across the village square. To me, a lapsed and inadequate Protestant, the intensely Catholic funeral service, with its incense and bells, was almost like a piece of theatre. The funeral oration was long and many famous men would have been well satisfied with its sincerity and eloquence. M. Lambert himself would have been pleased, though he would certainly never have dreamed of describing himself, as the priest did, as 'a member of the hard-working aristocracy of the soil'.

The Caumonts and other farmers helped Mme Lambert get in that year's harvest, but she knew that it was impossible for her and her daughter to continue farming. She rented the land on both farms to other farmers. More practical and less sensitive than her late husband, she persuaded the surly tenant to leave her mother-in-law's house, and soon sold it to a couple who worked in British television.

I had coveted the house myself, situated as it was in a sunny valley with a stream, and wooded hillsides above its cornfields, and at the end of a private road almost a kilometre long, but I had no money to spare. They got the bargain of the year and have restored the farmhouse, and converted a barn into another roomy cottage, installing a swimming pool and sunbathing terrace between the two. Mme Lambert remains in her own house on this side of the village and still has her kitchen garden, and her chickens, geese and ducks. She thinks, two years after her husband's death, that she may take a holiday. In more than twenty years of married life, she had only one day off. They spent a summer day at the coast, two hours' drive away, at the resort of Arcachon. She worried all day about getting back in time to milk the cows.

Grandmother Caumont was older than Mère Lambert but more active. She still lived in the room to which she had come as a young bride more than sixty years earlier, and where M. Caumont had been born. When we first arrived, old Mme Caumont cooked for the whole family, as well as providing meals, as is the custom here, for seasonal workers such as pruners and fruit-pickers. I never saw her in anything but the peasant black. Like her son she was of a calm, good-natured disposition and even in her mid-eighties she looked a strong, upright woman.

In the autumn after we arrived, still very much newcomers, we were invited to the wedding of M. Caumont's son. The marriage ceremony took place in a small and ancient church in a hamlet a few kilometres from the village. It was packed, mostly with farmers and their families, but M. Caumont has many contacts in the fruit industry and there were also business associates present. Like all marriages it was a happy occasion, and I remember most how astonished I was at the quality of the choral singing, which would have done credit to a trained choir. There was no choir, just the farmers and their wives, but in this part of France at least, the people, like the Welsh and the Russians, are natural singers.

There were far too many guests for the reception to be held in M. Caumont's house, but as it was October, usually serene and golden and warm in the south-west, drinks and food were to be served at tables neatly arranged under the canopy of the great barn. Unfortunately, October had decided, just for that Saturday, to become cold and windy, and the farmers' wives who had taken the rare opportunity to put on their best dresses and summery hats shivered in the first breath of winter. Their husbands looked uncomfortable in their suits and with collars and ties. Most men in the countryside of France have only one suit, which is dark, and which they buy for their own wedding and afterwards wear only at other weddings and at funerals. As they get older, work makes them more muscular and they put on weight, or they eat well and they put on weight, but they don't like to spend money on a new suit unless it is absolutely essential. So at all weddings and funerals there is a good display of jackets ready to burst at the seams, and the owners' discomfort is increased by the restriction around the neck. In most parts of France outside Paris, ties are reserved for politicians and television comperes and announcers; the farmer wears a tie only to church. As the Church itself admits that in France almost the only Christians left are what they call 'festive Christians', those who go to church only for weddings, baptisms and funerals, and at Easter and Christmas, the farmer never gets used to wearing a tie.

Grandmother Caumont, who was one of the few who still went to church almost every Sunday, lived to see her grandson happily married, and her first great-grandchildren toddling in the farm-yard. She died, after a short indisposition, at ninety-two, in the room which had been her bedroom for seventy years.

Chapter Seven

THE SHRIEKING FIREMAN AND OTHER WILDLIFE

One of the minor mysteries of life is that all animals, and even insects, seem to know when they are being watched. It was not long after the leaky roof incident that I began to experience this sensation. Marie-Anne had been quick to realise that I had unsuspected potential as a DIY man, and when my birthday came round a couple of months later I was presented with a power drill, and one of those ingenious workbenches which you can reassemble in all sorts of different positions. It was a big change. Up till then her attitude had been characterised by her reaction to an incident when we lived in Sussex by the sea. One dark and stormy night, the bathroom window, carelessly left open, blew off its hinges. In the morning, after a draughty wash and brush-up, I told Marie-Anne, who refused to get up to 'wash in a blizzard'. I had never fancied myself as a handyman, but I made temporary repairs with a piece of old linoleum and nails. She got up and we called a builder. When, two weeks later, he had not arrived, I offered to reglaze and refit the window myself. Marie-Anne begged me not to. 'You'll put yourself in hospital,' she said.

That had always been her opinion of my DIY talents, and it had rankled, but things were different now. So what had been the garage for M. Rambaud's paralysed American limousine was converted into a workshop, with the virgin bench in the middle, and with a good deal more bravado than confidence I became a handyman.

I had worked at the bench only a few times when a day came when I felt I was being watched. I looked around, but could see nothing. After a while the feeling returned. This time I looked up quickly and thought I saw something move near the rafters on the back wall. The third time I worked round slowly until I was facing that wall with my head still bent over the job and then gradually looked up. A small face dominated by large shiny eyes was watching me with interest from the top of the wall under the angle of the roof. I did not know what it was. I made an abrupt movement and it quickly disappeared. That end of the workshop was largely occupied by a concrete wine vat about ten feet long, six feet wide and six feet high, a monument to the elephantine thirst of some unknown predecessor. I fetched a pair of steps and, for the first time, climbed on top of this vat to investigate. I noticed that the angle between the top of the wall and the bottom of the roof had been at some time cemented up, but only partly, so that on the inside a long, narrow tunnel ran along the top of the wall. Whatever it was lived inside the tunnel, or at least used it.

I thought about the animals I had seen about the place. There were red squirrels in the copse by the river, and there was one that spent its time either in the chestnut tree in front of the house or in the lime tree behind it. There were various field mice, shrews and voles, but the face was too large for them, too big even for a large rat. Once I had gone down to the riverside on a summer morning soon after dawn, and had spotted a couple of coypus playing and doing their morning exercises on and around and under an old tree trunk fallen in the water near the bank, but the coypu is an aquatic animal not to be found in buildings. There was an old badger set down there, but M. Caumont told me it had been deserted for several years, so my visitor was not an adventurous badger. There were rabbits and hedgehogs but even I, with my limited knowledge of nature, felt that they would not be at home in the roof of a garage. There were birds of all kinds but those eyes were certainly not those of a bird. Thinking of birds I remembered that I had found some half shells of chicken eggs in odd places around the barn, which had mystified me, since the nearest hens were the best part of a quarter of a mile away at M. Lambert's farm.

Next time I saw him, I mentioned the mystery animal to him. 'Ceux sont des fouines,' he said at once. 'They are tree-martens. There are a lot of them in this area.' The tree-marten, I found out, is a close relative of the pine-marten, which exists in parts of Wales and Scotland. The tree-marten is rather like a weasel but larger, with handsome reddish-brown fur which is creamy on the underside. It has a pointed face with large brown eyes and an alert, interested expression. According to M. Lambert its chief enemy was the squirrel which it killed whenever it could catch one.

I told him about the eggshells. 'It's them without a doubt,' he said. 'They carry them in their mouth to where they want to eat them. Though, mind you, rats steal eggs, only they carry them in their front paws.'

Now that I knew what they were, I began to see them more often. Sometimes early in the morning I would disturb one in the orchard and watch it scooting between the trees towards the river. I had previously taken them for squirrels, because their coat is a similar colour to that of the red squirrel in Britain, but here the squirrel is a darker, richer red, and, though the marten has a bushy tail, it does not curl it up as the squirrel does when it stops. I solved the workshop problem by cementing up both ends of the tunnel, but this was only the beginning of a war which lasted two years.

The trouble came to a head when, having decided that we enjoyed having holiday visitors, we set about converting the fermette into another holiday cottage. In blocking the tunnel under the eaves, I had forgotten that the rafters in the garage communicated with the roof space above the ceiling of the fermette. One day I was standing in the fermette's ancient kitchen, wondering how to make the best use of the space, and how to solve several important problems, such as the fact that the walls were running with damp and encrusted with saltpetre, when my train of thought was interrupted by a commotion above my head.

These martens are, apparently, playful animals and it sounded to me as if they were enjoying their own version of five-a-side football in the roof, as they scampered and slid all over the ceiling with occasional squeaks of excitement. Though interesting, it was not the sort of performance that holiday visitors would be likely to appreciate particularly if it woke them from a sound sleep, as it certainly would have done. The martens had another serious disadvantage: they were filthy. They left their black droppings everywhere and particularly liked the white surround of the swimming pool and, as I soon learned, their actual base or nest stank like an overcrowded lion house in a badly run zoo. The problem was straightforward: it was holiday visitors or martens, and as the martens paid no rent and we needed the money, they would have to be evicted. As nobody but the martens had lived in the fermette for some fifty years, they were not going to go quietly. Another point which had to be taken into consideration was an ecological one. They are on the list of protected species.

But a year or so in France had been long enough for me to understand that, as far as the French are concerned, a regulation is something which you respect only until it begins to inconvenience you. I mentioned the difficulty to M. Caumont, who had the same attitude towards ecology as most French farmers. He had nothing against it unless it interfered with his farming. If he found too many rabbits among his young maize, he invited the local shooting club to have a day out. He agreed that no holiday visitor, not even an ardent naturalist, would want a tribe of martens in the immediate proximity of his bedroom, and suggested I should take the problem to the local veterinary surgeon who would probably have an answer.

He did. He agreed that something must be done, and could be done, but that it was strictly illegal and I must say nothing about it. He suggested that I should bring him half a dozen new laid eggs which he would inject with strychnine, and which I should take away and then, wearing gloves so that the animals would not scent human interference, place them in odd corners where the martens would be likely to find them. I carefully followed these instructions. All the eggs disappeared, and I heard no more football matches in the fermette roof space. I thought the problem was solved.

But the following spring when I went into the filtration room, which had been closed for the winter and was on the other side of the barn from the fermette, to check the installation before putting the swimming pool into use, I noticed at once the sickening smell and the black droppings. The martens were back. The only possible place for them in this lean-to building against the side of the barn was in the roof.

I went back to the vet, and to save myself a journey took the eggs with me. This time I saw his partner, who made no bones about the procedure except to tell me that it was illegal, and to charge me, with typical Gascon enterprise, five times what his partner had asked the year before. I considered this an exaggerated rise even in this esoteric sector of the economy and mentioned it to him. 'Ah, bon,' he said with an easy smile, 'Let's call it fifty francs, then,' so knocking it down to only about twice the previous year's bill.

Once again the remedy seemed to be effective. We had a family staying in the pigeonnier in which there were two young boys who enjoyed using the table tennis area we had arranged at one end of the pool. One afternoon about a week later, they stopped playing as I walked by and the older one said, 'There isn't half a pong round here. We think it's that thing up there,' pointing to the roof of the barn.

What they were pointing at was a dead tree-marten. 'I'll get rid of it,' I said.

I found a fairly large plastic shopping bag, put on a pair of old gloves, fetched a ladder and climbed on to the roof, wishing I had put a clothes peg on my nose. I was surprised at the size of the body, noticeably larger than our fully grown cat, Cleo, and weighing about four kilos. As it happened I had a fairly lively bonfire going, so I consigned it to the flames, and that was almost the end of the marten story, except for a postscript which I shall tell you about later.

I noticed once or twice when telling my English visitors about the martens that a rather dazed and vacant expression came over their faces as I talked about how they chased the squirrels through the tree-tops and seemed to play football in the roof space. Then it dawned on me that they thought I was talking about house-martins, those charming, swallow-like birds that herald summer. There are martins among the many different species of birds here, and we notice them every summer because the occasional sight of them dipping and swooping just above the surface of the swimming pool is a reliable sign that bad weather is not far away. I have never found out where they nest.

The barn is the obvious place, but they do not use it; perhaps the owls make them nervous. I am not an amateur ornithologist, and I take no special interest in birds, but those of our visitors who do soon become enthusiastic about the variety of species to be seen here. The hoopoe and the cuckoo arrive within a few days of each other every April. The hoopoe is always first, and is as easily recognisable by its repeated onomatopoeic call as is the cuckoo. I often see hoopoes on the ground or in flight, but I have not yet seen a cuckoo. A pair of green woodpeckers live somewhere near our garden where I often see them on the lawn. Buzzards wheel in the sky above the orchard and perch at the highest point of the acacias and poplars, and there are also black and red kites. Down by the river, kingfishers flash gaudily along the bank just above the water, and there are herons and night herons, and at the top of the bank in a shrubbery of nut trees and elderberries, nightingales sing.

Sometimes in the late summer twilight the owls swoop down from the cross-beam of the barn and whoosh low overhead. All year round we hear them from time to time as they hunt. They are not the polite tu-whit tu-whoo sort of owl, instead they give vent to a horrifying, drawn-out screech that chills the blood. One lady guest who had not been warned and was peacefully admiring the moonlit summer sky came rushing in, visibly frightened, saying, 'There's something horrible out there.' There are many magpies and rooks, and we often see jays in the orchard. Golden orioles sometimes come to feed on the lawn in front of the house, and among the smaller birds there are tree-creepers, hedge sparrows, and several kinds of finch. A retired scientist who lives further downriver says that he has listed more than fifty species of birds, including migrant species, in the river valley.

There is also a remarkable variety of insects, including great green grasshoppers, colourful dragonflies, many kinds of butterfly, carpenter bees, bumble bees and wasps. Probably because of the quantity of available fruit in the orchards, we are rarely bothered by a wasp in the house, but I noticed when having a look at the roof space in the fermette, after the martens had left, that there were several wasp nests on the underside of the tiles and rafters, and I thought this was another form of life which visitors would not appreciate. I mentioned it to Marcel, a young man who came to help around the place one afternoon a week. He had started life as an industrial chemist in the north of France, but did not like it and had become a forester instead. He was responsible for the maintenance of several woods in southern Dordogne, and did other outdoor jobs of all sorts on different properties in his spare time. He seemed to know something about everything, and was remarkably competent and reliable.

For wasps, however, he referred us to the 'pompiers' – the fire brigade. I can speak only for this region of France but here the 'pompiers' are highly regarded men-of-all-work. They do not do much rescuing of cats up trees, because the average French countryman thinks that cats can look after themselves and if a cat can get up a tree, it can get down, sooner or later. But other problems of all sorts, dangerous buildings, cars in rivers or ditches, fallen trees, stray animals, insect plagues, and a host of other things, all come within their province, especially when the problem is above ground level. They also attend the scene of road accidents. One of the reasons that help is soon at hand when road accidents occur is that both the police and the fire brigade are advised at the same time, and it is a matter of honour and rivalry who gets there first. The firemen are the usual winners.

Marie-Anne rang them up and told them about the wasps. Yes, they said, they would be happy to help. In due course they arrived in a bright red van with its oompah going full blast, which to me seemed hardly necessary for a few wasps.

There were two of them, one young, resplendent in what seemed like a brand new uniform, with an eager look about him, the other old enough to be his father, tough and taciturn. I noticed that he gave Marie-Anne an odd, sideways look as she explained the problem to them. 'We'll have a look at it,' was all he said.

'It's our job to help people,' said the eager young man. 'Sometimes we have to deal with tragedy, save lives, put ourselves at risk. It's all in the public interest.' He seemed to be paraphrasing a recruitment speech. 'This will be nothing compared with some of the things we have to do.'

'Better get ready,' said the older one, climbing into the van. We waited, and a few minutes later they emerged looking like spacemen, covered in protective clothing, and the younger one already had his face mask in position, and was carrying a heavy cylinder.

'What are you going to do?' said Marie-Anne suspiciously, looking at the cylinder.

'Fumigate it,' said the older one. 'That's what we always do. This thing blows out a fine spray of fuel oil. Nothing better. They won't come back for years.'

'Neither will my clients,' said Marie-Anne. 'You can't do that. That smell gets everywhere, you just can't get rid of it.' This had been a sore point with Marie-Anne since the time when the delivery man had allowed the fuel tank to overflow in the cellar. My head injury, soon healed, concerned her less than the fact that the smell of the fuel had persisted in the house for months.

He looked at Marie-Anne again with that curious resigned expression, as if he had been expecting her to make difficulties.

'Put it away,' he told the lad. 'We'll have to collect them.' Looking crestfallen the new fireman put the cylinder back in the van.

We showed them how to get into the roof of the fermette.

'Have you got a ladder?' asked tough and taciturn.

I found him an extending ladder, and we left them to it.

'Firemen without a ladder,' Marie-Anne muttered to herself, as we made our way back to the house.

'Why was he looking at you like that?' I asked her.

'He was the one I saw when I went to ask about the swimming pool.'

'Ah, that explains it.'

The story was this. When we had finally got the swimming pool looking like a swimming pool instead of a mysterious and dirty hole in the ground, there was the question of filling it. We had no mains water, but there was a well in the orchard and a spring under the canopy of the barn. Both, according to M. Rambaud, were inexhaustible but we had had a long dry spell and were afraid the well would run dry, before the pool was full, and leave us with no water for the house. Our anxiety was based on the fact that the pool was large, nowhere more than five feet deep but fifty metres long. It would hold a lot of water. Someone told us that the fire brigade would fill swimming pools, so one day when we were in town shopping Marie-Anne went into the fire station to ask them.

'Yes,' said the tough and taciturn fireman. 'We do that sometimes. What is its capacity?'

'Three hundred and twenty cubic metres.' She had been prepared for this question.

'With respect, madame, I think you must mean thirty-two cubic metres.'

'No, three hundred and twenty. I have it written down somewhere. It's fifty metres long.'

Tough and taciturn paused. 'We do have a water tanker, madame. We do sometimes fill children's swimming pools, those round inflatable ones. But our tanker contains three cubic metres of water, so we should need at least a hundred journeys to fill your pool, and as we have many other things to do it might take a considerable time. I regret it is not practical, and also expensive.'

'I see. Thank you.'

This had been two years previously but the fireman had obviously not forgotten it.

We had not gone far from the fermette when we heard a shriek that would have done credit to a mammoth barn owl. It was followed by an agonised groan.

'What happened? What have they done?' cried Marie-Anne, and we hurried back to the fermette.

'What happened?' she asked tough and taciturn who was standing in the passage looking up into the open loft space, and laughing quietly to himself.

'He was frightened by a mouse, that's all.'

Apparently our heroic young recuit, ready to risk his life in the public interest, had been startled by a mouse, shrieked and jumped back and in the same instant hit his head on a low rafter. We could not see him, but we heard his voice.

'It's all right. I was taken by surprise. It was only a mouse.'

'Good job it was not a tree-marten,' I said to Marie-Anne.

The average wasp nest is about the size of a clenched fist or smaller, and when they came to report that they had finished, about an hour later, they had a sack with, they said, about fifty nests in it.

'Just as well you called us, madame,' said tough and taciturn to Marie-Anne. 'Give a spray round with an insecticide aerosol and you shouldn't be troubled.' His colleague's behaviour seemed to have cheered him up quite a bit.

'What do we owe you?'

The young man opened his mouth, but a glance from his colleague silenced him.

'There's no official charge,' he said.

'Well, anyway you have been a great help, and there must be a fire brigade charity,' Marie-Anne said giving him a hundred-franc note. He seemed to think this right and proper, and they climbed into their red van and drove off. We heard the siren start before they were out of sight.

Chapter Eight

WHAT ABOUT MY HOUSE?

When we had first arrived and Marie-Anne had said, looking at M. Rambaud's kitchen and downstairs bathroom, that it would all have to go, I had agreed. Even if I had foreseen the difficulties, I would not have dared to voice them. One of the basic rules of happy marriage is to let your wife have what she wants in matters of kitchens and bathrooms, and a good deal else besides. But M. Rambaud's version of these necessities looked like neglected exhibits in some museum devoted to nineteenth-century living in backward parts of the French countryside, so when the pigeonnier conversion was finished and Marie-Anne said, 'Now, what about my kitchen?' I knew what she meant.

It seemed simple after all. The space was a plain rectangle divided into one-third bathroom, two-thirds kitchen with a wall separating them and a communicating door. The bathroom had a French door, opening on to a sort of terrace garden behind the house enclosed by a laurel hedge between the house and the orchard, and a window facing the fermette. The kitchen had a French door opening on to the garden at the front of the house, but no other window.

Knock down the dividing wall, take out the bathroom fittings, put in washing machine, oven, and what have you, and there you were, we thought. Easy.

We were perhaps misled by the apparent ease with which 'the boys', on the Godfather's instructions, had put in the replacement bathroom as an extension on the other side of the house, and created a new drainage system for the pigeonnier. But in that case the new bathroom extension had been built outside the main house, and the work on the door to it in the corner of the bedroom, the removal of the fireplace and the smoothing of the bedroom wall, was all that was actually done from inside the house. Most of this work had been done as if by magic in one day. But all the work to turn the decrepit old kitchen and bathroom into a modern farmhouse kitchen would be done in our own living quarters.

Chaos was come again. There were one or two points which had not occurred to us. We soon realised, for example, that a two-hundred-litre hot water tank would not look quite right in the corner of a fitted kitchen. It was removed and placed, logically enough, in the attic above the bedroom in the corner nearest the new bathroom. Getting it up there, around the sharp angles of our narrow old staircase, and through three dwarf doorways, was a circus performance accompanied by cracked heads, jarred elbows, and a succession of unmentionable French phrases which were new to me and had not been part of Marie-Anne's convent education.

Then came the question of disposing of the bath itself and the hand-basin, the bidet and the loo with the orange plastic seat. Much to my surprise both Marie-Anne and daughter Ari, who was staying with us at the time, discovered a sudden attraction to the bath.

'It's lovely,' said Ari. 'You must keep it. It's the latest thing in Habitat. Put it in the upstairs bathroom and throw out the one that's there.' Habitat was all the rage at the time, and Marie-Anne was easily convinced. I could see that it had possibilities. It looked like a line illustration from a department store catalogue of the Edwardian era and it had one quality long forgotten in modern baths – it was deep. It was the sort of bath where you could get the back of your neck and your knees under water at the same time with no trouble at all, a bath where you could do what can't be done in the average modern bath; you could wallow. Another thing in its favour was that it was white, not some sickly shade of green or pink.

'All right,' I said. More complications, I thought. Having seen the torture of getting the hot water tank up the stairs, I wondered how they would manage with a solid cast-iron bath which was larger and twice as heavy. I could see them having to take the banisters down.

M. de Cany not being on the spot, we put the question to M. Bien-venue.

'Hah!' he said, tapping the old bath with a certain amount of respect. 'They don't make them like that any more. They don't even make cast iron like that. Pre-war, that is.'

We asked him if it could be fitted upstairs.

'Fitted, yes,' he said, and then metaphorically poured cold water on the whole idea. 'Oh, yes, fitted, but fill a bath like that with water upstairs, and likely as not, it will fall through the floor. Empty bath, not much use, I dare say.' His tone somehow suggested that, though he put in baths for others, he still had to be convinced that they were much use in any circumstances.

'You could strengthen the floor,' said my daughter, not easily beaten. No response. 'Well, keep it in the barn then. When I get a flat of my own, you can bring it to London in the car.' We had swopped the little Alfa for a more practical estate car to help transport cement, wood, paint and all the etceteras necessary for renovation. It would take a lot but not, I thought, a cast-iron bath.

Well, we did keep it in the barn for a couple of years. In the end we gave it to Marcel. What he did with I don't know. Possibly sold it to his brother, Yves. A surprising number of men in this part of France build their own houses, and Yves was one of them. Most of them take about eighteen months with the help of relatives and friends, but Yves has been building his house for several years and it is not finished. He is a first-class workman but, unfortu-nately, is never satisfied, and pulls it down almost as quickly as he puts it up. This gets him into trouble with the authorities, because there are grants for people who build their own homes, and inspectors come round to check that you have actually spent the money on building materials, and not on booze and fancy women. I don't think there was the slighest danger of this as far as Yves was concerned. His wife was a nursing sister and it was Yves who stayed home and divided his time between cooking and cleaning and building their new home. As far as she was concerned this gave him a lot of free time, and she watched him as carefully as a cat watches a mouse. When he did a small job for us, she turned up unexpectedly one afternoon to check where he was, and what he was doing, and what Madame was like. So Yves may have had the bath, or Marcel, who, in tune with his back-to-nature lifestyle, kept a cow and some sheep, may have turned it into a drinking trough. Or he may have used it as a bath.

Then there was the matching hand-basin and matching bidet, which Marie-Anne wanted to put on the local rubbish dump. But I was fascinated by the hand-basin. M. Bienvenue did not say, but might well have said, 'That's another thing they don't make like that any more.' The basin itself was big enough to sail a model yacht in, and it had a flat surround back, front and sides, about six inches wide and very practical for putting down glasses, shaving brushes, aerosols, hair rollers, and all the things that you can never find space for around modern hand-basins. From a splash of scarlet nail varnish in one corner I guessed that it might have been a left-over from the lady from the Moulin Rouge. Anyway, I decided to keep them, and put them away in the barn.

Christmas was coming and all hell broke loose in an attempt to get Marie-Anne a new kitchen in time for the holiday. Two masons removed the kitchen range, its graveyard marble, and its flue, took out the ancient gas stove, and knocked down the wall between the two rooms, creating a heap of rubble and a cloud of dust. Fortunately, the door between the kitchen and our living room had been temporarily sealed up in anticipation of this. When the wall was down and the dust had settled, there was of course a gap in the ceiling where it had been. The ceiling, as is often the case in south-west France, was of the tongued and grooved pine strips called 'lambris'. The bathroom section had been painted green, and the kitchen section pink. With the wall between them we had not paid much attention to this. Without it, we realised fairly quickly that a modern fitted kitchen, even a farmhouse kitchen, with half the ceiling bright green and the other half pastel pink might be considered eccentric as well as unpleasant. This problem was eventually resolved by the painter, a M. Filloneau, who might himself have been considered eccentric by some, since he travelled around in an ancient and massive Peugeot which worked not on petrol or diesel fuel but with gas, supplied from a huge container on its roof. I have never seen its like since.

A typical Gascon town house.

But first, there was the ten-inch gap between the ceilings to deal with. While it is clearly not true to say that M. Loubradou, the master carpenter, had old oak beams coming out of his ears, he was certainly never at a loss for one, and he had soon found and fitted one so that it looked as if it had always been there.

With some tolerance it could now be said that we had a beamed kitchen, and we were still keen on having what, although fitted with the approved modern labour-saving devices, would look like a farmhouse kitchen. We decided, after hesitating about the expense, that the one thing that would do this convincingly would be a traditional, log-burning, stone fireplace, taking up the end wall of what had been the bathroom, and was now the end wall of the kitchen.

The French love these traditional fireplaces and refuse to abandon them, even in the most modern houses. Every region of France has its own traditional design, and people who move into Brittany from Burgundy will put a typically Burgundian fireplace in their brand new house, and Bretons will put a Breton fireplace in their holiday home in Provence or Languedoc. The fireplace has become a minor art form in France, and has also acquired considerable snob value as a symbol of comfort, solidity and affluence. When newly-weds acquire their first home, an impressive fireplace is high on the list of essentials, and no builder of mass market housing could possibly hope for success, even in the south of France, without including a traditional fireplace in his price. Even the well-to-do follow the trend. I remember that Marie-Anne's father, who lived in a splendid apartment in the Avenue Hoche, the Park Lane of Paris, had an imposing fireplace, in his case largely brick-built, with recesses on either side for logs. No fire had ever been lit in it, and in the twenty years I knew him, the same sanitised logs all of equal diameter remained neatly stacked on either side.

But Marie-Anne, who feels the cold, meant ours for possible use. 'You never know,' she said. 'It might get cold even here, remember that time in Cyprus.' We had once been in Cyprus in April and had shivered in a villa without heating. 'And if there's a power cut and the central heating goes off, we shall have at least one room where we can be warm.' It was a remark that turned out to be prophetic.

As it happened, the chief plasterer, M. Brehat, was also an expert on the construction of traditional fireplaces. As soon as I mentioned it, he made a phone call and whisked me away into town to the house of a bewildered old widow for whom he had recently installed a fine stone fireplace.

'This is the sort of thing you want,' he said. And he was quite right, it was.

'I'm very pleased with it,' said the old lady. 'It draws beautifully.'

No real fireplace in Aquitaine is worth the name unless it will comfortably take logs at least a metre long. However, despite their fondness for imposing fireplaces, one thing the typical Gascon farmer does not like to see is a blazing fire. When he looks into the flames, what he sees is money burning. So, when you go into a genuine farm kitchen, what you normally see is a miserable fire with one large log glowing slightly on the underside.

No sooner had M. Brehat marked out the wall for what he was going to do than we found that beneath the old plaster there was an attractive wall of natural stones of all shapes and sizes interspersed here and there with flat red clay bricks about an inch thick.

'That would look nice on either side of the chimney,' said Marie-Anne, ominously. All these traditional fireplaces have a projecting chimney which continues up to the ceiling.

So we had carpenters making holes in the side walls to take the ends of the beam which would mask the hole where the wall had been, while M. Brehat dodged in and out measuring up for the fireplace, and M. Loubradou and his assistant circled about measuring up for Marie-Anne's fitted kitchen and arguing with her about what should go where, and how it should be plumbed in, while the masons removed the pile of rubble from the wall, while the plumber said he couldn't plumb anything in without drains and he couldn't find the drains to the main house, and the electrician swerved in and out like a rugby scrum-half, trying to agree where the new power points for kettle, washing machine, eye-level oven and dishwasher should go and warning us that it would all fuse anyway. We were soon obliged to abandon our house in favour of the pigeonnier for meals and an occasional rest.

Somehow in the midst of chaos things advanced. The fireplace and chimney were completed, except for the final plastering of the chimney itself. The Godfather pointed out that the wall would look nothing unless it was cleaned and the joints between the stones were repointed. He sent in the 'boys' to deal with this. I remember a day when the telepathic twins worked shoulder to shoulder in the corner on one side of the chimney, picking out the old joints to make them deep enough for the new mortar, while a third mason did the same job on the other side of the chimney.

This third man, who appeared only a few times, was remarkably corpulent and talkative. He had suffered some time previously an accident at work which had incapacitated him to an extent which had long been debated, with him on one side and the doctors, the social security woman and the Minister of Health on the other. He had apparently made a particular enemy of 'the bitch' at the social security. Occasionally, he tapped his chisel with his hammer and a small piece of mortar fell away, but most of the time he had his back to the wall while he recited the saga of his 'accident de travail' with an interminable succession of I said, she said, I told her, I wrote to the Ministry, they didn't reply, what do the doctors know?, I said, she said, I told her and so on. Everybody ignored him. Pierre and Jean, as ever, remained silent, except that Pierre looked round once, his glance taking in the chisel in one hand and the hammer in the other and the back to the wall, and said, 'And when did you get back to work then?'

'Three weeks ago.'

'Ah, bon,' said Pierre, turning back.

M. Brehat's plasterer, now repairing the damage to the side walls, had brought a small radio with him which in self-defence he turned up loud. Nobody took any notice, least of all the corpulent one, who, having been shamed into two minutes' work by Pierre's attitude, then turned round and continued talking, 'I forgot to tell you . . .'

As soon as the masons had finished repointing the wall, they went outside and dug a trench in the garden behind the house across the full width of the building, in an effort to find the drains.

In some miraculous way they completely failed and reported that there was no hint of a drain anywhere, which meant, of course, that the new kitchen would have to have new drains. When I suggested that there must have been drains somewhere, the Godfather, having correctly divined that I was not going to start digging trenches everywhere myself, looked me straight in the eye and said, 'Ah, but where?' and then explained how simple it would be to connect the new kitchen to the new system already installed for the pigeonnier. I retired, defeated again.

While this piece of Gascon enterprise was going on outside, the plasterer had returned to finish off the chimney, two electricians were doing the rewiring and M. Loubradou's carpenters were starting on the fitted cupboards, some of which would house the various appliances. In the midst of all this Marie-Anne found the plasterer moving his hands over the plaster of the finished chimney like an amateur hypnotist trying to weave a spell. Looking closer she saw that he was actually moving his fingers in the still wet plaster, leaving wavy marks all over it.

'But I wanted it smooth,' she said.

'But this is authentic,' said the plasterer, without stopping. 'This is what we call the Périgord style. I was taught how to do this by my father and grandfather.' He sounded hurt, and Marie-Anne did not insist. She had been impressed with his relentless speed and efficiency when he had worked in the pigeonnier, stripped to his jean shorts, in the hottest days of the summer. 'I've never seen anyone work harder than that young man,' she told me. 'And he looks like Tarzan.' So she let him go on weaving his spell, and we have a chimney 'a la manière du Périgord'.

In the end the kitchen was almost finished. Nothing remained to do but the floors and the ceiling. The fitted shelves and cupboards were there and the appliances hidden behind them so that when the cupboard doors were shut the kitchen looked both spacious and neat. This system of hiding washing machines etc. in cupboards was relatively new in France then and even the resourceful M. Loubradou had not foreseen the possible problems, one of which we discovered some time later when we wanted to get at the back of the machine to clean the intake. The washing machine was so neatly enclosed by the cupboard and the work surface above it that it was impossible to move it out to get at the back. I solved this problem by easing the work surface up a few fractions of an inch, as gently as I could, with a car jack mounted on a stack of bricks.

Another thing which did not turn out quite right was the oven. Marie-Anne had set her heart on an eye-level oven with all its advantages, including no stooping to take things out. But we realised, just before it was to be installed, that from much of the kitchen it would effectively block the view of the wall which had been so laboriously and expensively revealed ... Out went the eye-level oven and into what would have been the cupboard below, came an ordinary oven. No problem, except that the back of that cupboard was where the electrician had already installed his complicated fuse panel, so that when a fuse blows, which happily has not often happened, we have to take the oven out before we can put in a new fuse.

When M. Filloneau arrived in his motorised gas-bag to fit our vinyl floor with its design of tiles – we were running out of money and had decided that we could not afford the real thing – the first thing he said as he looked round the kitchen was, 'Very nice, but I should have been here first.'

'Oh, why?' asked Marie-Anne, politely.

'The flooring should go from wall to wall, and all that stuff should be on top of it.' He paused. 'Ah, well perhaps it doesn't matter.' He had realised that there was no question of taking 'all that stuff' out, and we understand now that he said no more because he saw no point in frightening us.

It did matter, as we discovered about eighteen months later, when the washing machine flooded and some of the water seeped under the vinyl floor, part of which has been steadily changing colour ever since.

However, when M. Filloneau finished the floor and stepped back and said, 'Good. That's that, then,' it looked very good. But he had hardly straightened his back before Marie-Anne said, 'We can't leave the ceiling like that.'

M. Filloneau considered it. 'Indeed, it does look curious.' Pause. 'A white ceiling looks good in a kitchen.'

'We thought the best solution would be to strip it and restain the lambris in a natural wood colour,' I suggested hopefully, 'but I don't suppose you could get that old paint off.' Like all true professionals M. Filloneau could not resist a challenge.

'Oh, I could strip it off, all right,' he said. 'Long job, though.'

'All right, then, M. Filloneau, we'll leave it to you,' Marie-Anne said. 'I have seen how thorough you are, I'm sure you'll make a first-class job of it.'

M. Filloneau made no protest at this overt flattery, and he did do a good job. Except that when it came to restaining the lambris in the usual chestnut colour, which is what they had been before being painted, in his determination to be thorough, he also stained the natural oak beam.

'But I wanted it left as it was,' cried Marie-Anne. 'You've made it look like plastic.'

A number of emotions passed rapidly over M. Filloneau's work-worn face, ending in resignation.

'It's not dry. I can try to take it off.' If he had said, I can try to lift the Eiffel Tower, it would have been in the same tone of voice. But he did try, and he was ninety per cent successful, so that our old oak beam has only the merest tinge of reddish brown.

When it was finished, the only thing the kitchen lacked was ordinary furniture, a kitchen table and chairs. We looked around for something which would leave adequate space for easy movement all round it, and that would look right with the fireplace and the stone wall. After wandering patiently round one of those huge furniture hypermarkets which exist on the outskirts of every French town, we found a solid oak table which looked like an antique but was new and was just what we wanted, except that it was too large. Noticing that we had stopped for some time in front of it, the salesman came across.

'That's what we would like,' I said, 'but it is too big.' Remembering the form in London furniture shops, I expected him to start praising a smaller table somewhere else in the shop. He did not. Instead he said, 'Give me the measurements you want and I'll have it made for you.'

'Exactly the same?'

'Exactly, but the size you want.'

'How much?'

'The same price. You pay a deposit, and I'll order it. They are made by an artisan in the Pyrenees. It's all the same to him whether he makes it for me or for you.'

It took about a month, but we received a beautifully made table in solid Pyrenean oak, a table which takes two strong men to lift it, and which will last as long as the house, and which, like the oak beam above, looks as if it was always there.

And so, having exhausted our patience, our strength and our money, we decided to enjoy life in our renovated house for a few months before doing anything more.

Chapter Nine

DANGEROUS CURVES

One thing that anyone who comes to live in the countryside of France has to come to terms with very quickly is the crucial importance of the motor car. There are very large areas in which there is no effective public transport, neither buses nor trains. Of course, French rail services are efficient, clean, comfortable and invariably on time, but they operate almost entirely on long distance routes between major towns. There are many towns with no railway station at all. There are useful domestic air services, but the towns with an airport are even fewer than those with stations. Except for the buses that take children to school, bus services are almost non-existent. Marie-Anne, who dearly loved going for long rides on London buses, watching and listening to the pounding life of the city, took a long time to get used to never seeing a bus on the roads. The combination of long distances, which mean high running costs, and a scattered population makes them uneconomical. So, having arrived at a railway station or an airport, you must carry on by car.

If you live in a village and want to go to the nearest town, you must go by car. You go from small town to small town by car. You go to work by car. You shop by car. You visit friends and relatives by car. You take the children on holiday, to the mountains or the beaches, by car. What you do not do, if you are the average French countryman, is to motor for pleasure. If a French farmer said to his wife, 'It's a nice afternoon, let's go for a drive,' she would be tempted to send for the doctor. The car, to a French countryman, is a machine which gets him where he needs to go. The idea of spending money on idling about the countryside admiring the scenery is totally foreign to him.

So almost every French family has at least one car, and they use them a lot, for everything except pleasure. In general, the French are good, alert drivers, though perhaps not as good as they believe themselves to be. Compared with Britain there are about five times as many miles of roads in France for roughly the same number of cars, but, despite all this extra space, the number of people killed annually on French roads is more than double what it is in Britain. A lot of the trouble comes from an aggressive and irresponsible minority. Some of them seem intent on demonstrating that their cars, however old and small, are considerably faster than Jaguars, Mercedes or Alfa Romeos, among others. Drivers of this sort also like to demonstrate that, unlike most of us, they can see through thick fog, and that their cars, unlike some, do not skid on icy roads. Unfortunately, these demonstrations are often unsuccessful, resulting in regular pile-ups involving fifty or sixty cars on the autoroutes, and countless crashes into roadside trees. The same kind of driver believes that wet roads are just as safe as dry roads, and that following ten feet behind the motorist in front at fifty miles an hour is perfectly safe, especially with only one hand on the wheel and the other, on which a gold wrist-watch is de rigueur, dangling casually outside the window. They also make it a point of honour to take up two-thirds of all narrow country roads and not to budge in the face of oncoming traffic. But probably the most dangerous driver in the world is the hungry provincial Frenchman on his way home to lunch. They will scream past you with inches to spare and a hundred metres further on slam on the brakes, swerve into their driveway and stop. I try not to be on the roads during the half hour after the town siren sounds for lunch, and also late at night when there are a great many accidents due to drunken driving, though the fines and consequences for convicted offenders are now severe.

One Saturday afternoon in late spring, about a year after we arrived here, we were sitting on the terrace behind the house, enjoying the warmth of the sun and listening to the bees in the lime tree, and not talking much, except for a contented phrase or two about how pleased we were with the way the pigeonnier had turned out, and wondering how to set about finding our first holiday clients. Apart from the bees and the crickets, and the distant rumble of a tractor somewhere on the other side of the river, the afternoon was enfolded in a golden silence, that pause when the working world takes a breather before setting about its weekend activities. Suddenly there was a loud, metallic bang, accompanied by the crash of broken glass.

'What on earth was that?' said Marie-Anne.

'It sounded like . . . Better look, come on.' We dashed round to the front of the house. We could see at once that there was a commotion at the road end of our drive. Two cars had stopped there, and one of them was in the ditch. We ran up the drive. Two men, one fat, one thin, somehow reminiscent of Laurel and Hardy, were sitting side by side on the grass, conscious but completely dazed, with blood streaming down their faces, and an almost visible halo of strip cartoon stars around their heads. It was easy to see what had happened. Our entrance is situated towards the end of a long, deceptive bend which seems too gentle to call for a reduction in speed. Unfortunately this is not the case if you are travelling too fast to begin with, for then the road continues with its bend and the car continues in a straight line and dives into the ditch and is abruptly stopped by the stonework of the little bridge which crosses it into our drive. The two men, however, had gone further, sailing through the windscreen on to the grass on the other side of the ditch.

It was only a small car, but three people, including two girls holding posies, scrambled out of the back of it and up the side of the ditch, fussed and shaken, but apparently unharmed. From the car behind men in suits and more girls in long dresses had emerged. It was a wedding party.

Marie-Anne went back to the house to telephone the police and the ambulance service. I stayed to see if any help was needed. There was not much I could do. Sangfroid is not a widely spread characteristic among the French. Everybody was talking at once, mostly in shrieked accusations. Nobody seemed much concerned with the men on the grass, once it had been established that they were both apparently not seriously hurt. One man went and stood in front of them and shouted invective at them, particularly the fat one, using all kinds of picturesque French swear words. What he seemed to be saying in essence was, 'Look what you've done to my car, you stupid fool. That's going to cost hundreds to put right. It will never be the same again. Did I say or didn't I, that you were in no fit state to drive?'

'Never mind your car, look at him,' shouted a woman, whom I supposed to be the guilty driver's wife. 'Anyway, you're insured, I suppose?'

'Insured? Of course I'm not bloody insured.'

'Then you are as stupid as he is. And just as drunk. If you'd been in front, you'd be in the ditch.' This bit of insurmountable feminine logic was strongly supported by other members of the group, and brought the car owner to near apoplexy. And so it went on.

I stayed until the police arrived, and having given my name and the official address of the scene of the accident, left them all to it.

It was the first of seven similar accidents to date on the three hundred metres of country road bordering our fields, none quite so drastic, but several involving cars upside down in the ditch. All the country roads in the neighbourhood are lined by deep drainage ditches to take away storm water which otherwise lies too long on the almost impermeable clay soil. It is a commonplace to see cars in ditches anywhere in the region.

Then there was the day a serious young army officer came to the door.

'Excuse me,' he said, in French. 'We are on manoeuvres here. I have too many tanks. They are blocking the road. Can I park some in your drive?'

'I suppose so,' I said, also in French. 'As long as you don't block it. How many?'

'Ah. You are Eengleesh. I am speaking Eengleesh. I know ze accent.' He thought for a moment. 'Four will be enough.'

'Oh, that will be all right,' I said in English.

'It is very good. Tank you. Tank you very much.'

That was soon after 10 a.m. They stayed there, leaning on the tanks and talking, until the midday hooter announced that it was lunchtime. The crews climbed into the tanks and trundled off. It didn't do the gravel drive much good.

'If that's manoeuvres,' said Marie-Anne, 'I wonder what they do when they are not busy?'

Despite the catalogue of hazards and accidents, it is fair to say that there are few, if any, countries in the world where motoring is a greater pleasure than in France, and unlike most of the local residents Marie-Anne and I make the most of it. We like to get in the car and drive off, sometimes with no particular destination in mind. We may look for a new restaurant for lunch, or go back to one that we liked, perhaps months previously, or we may just take a picnic. When we do this we are enjoying a part of the answer to one of the questions we are most often asked by visitors. It comes in various forms – 'How on earth did you land up here?' – 'How did you find this wonderful place?' – 'What made you come here, I mean nobody has ever heard of it?' – 'Why did you choose a place so far from everywhere?'

I am not sure what the lady who asked this last question meant by 'everywhere'. Perhaps Paris or Monte Carlo, or Cannes, or Deauville or Le Touquet. It is true that none of those places is handy to us but, as I explained to her, there are very few areas of France with such a variety of scenery and interest within easy reach, and I listed some of the attractions for her.

In the immediate locality the valleys of the big rivers are wide, flat and fertile, but in the hills on either side there are dozens of small valleys, like lush Devon combes, watered by little brooks or streams. During our first exploratory visit we had stayed for a few days in a cottage converted from a disused water-mill in one of these hidden valleys. It was an idyllic spot, with an old garden, long abandoned, where the long grass was tangled with wild flowers, and forgotten rambler roses flowered in a mass of old man's beard, but we could not get used to the incessant rush, night and day, of the water beneath the living-room floor. So we left, having noted from the bare floors and very basic furniture, that there might be a gap at the top end of the market in French holiday cottages.

In some of these valleys there is nothing but a farm or two, in others tiny villages nestle, secretive and half-forgotten. They are often named after long-neglected saints, St Julien, St Colombe, St Sardos. Who were they? The roads that linked their villages are still only lanes, often grass-grown in the middle, with overgrown banks where summer bees drone among the wild flowers. At St

Le Pont Valentré at Cahors.

Sardos, a few miles from where I am writing, I doubt if any of the hundred or so inhabitants of this sleepy, attractive little village know that it was here that the first skirmish of the Hundred Years War took place. There is certainly no Café de la Guerre de Cent Ans to attract tourists, as there probably would be, if anyone knew. St Sardos actually stands on a hill overlooking a wide valley. It still has a few decrepit fourteenth-century houses, but the old church, the initial cause of the dispute, has crumbled away with its history, and has been replaced by an ordinary nineteenth-century version.

Further away to the west are the vineyards of the Bordeaux region, and the huge forest of the Landes, the largest in Europe, and the great golden sand beaches of the Atlantic coast. To the north there is Dordogne, including the Périgord Noir and all its prehistoric caves, and the old town of Sarlat. To the east is Cahors and the picturesque upper valley of the Lot, and further on Auvergne and the magnificent scenery of the Massif Central. To the south-east lie Toulouse, Albi, Carcassonne and the Mediterranean coast, nearest at Narbonne Plage. Due south the road leads direct to the Pyrenees and Spain. We are in the middle of all these places as the hub is in the middle of a wheel. Leaving after breakfast, we can reach any one of them in time for lunch, an afternoon on the beach, or a visit to the local sights, and be back home for supper. The longest of these journeys is that to Narbonne Plage, but even there we can be swimming in the Med a little more than three hours after leaving home.

All these places are linked by a magnificent road network which offers a variety of routes from any A to any B. As the average French driver does not consider motoring in terms of pleasure, he invariably uses the most direct and economical main road route. When they go on holiday, for winter sports, August sun and school half-term weeks, the French all go together on the same days and use only the main roads, so that holiday traffic jams have become a national pastime. At other times roads between towns, to the coast or to the mountains carry the lightest of traffic, and there are many secondary roads which are never busy at any time of year. The idea of a three-hour drive can be daunting in some parts of Britain, but in the great south-west it's a question of rolling along in comfort, unstressed, and it's easy to find beautiful picnic stops, or pleasant hotels or restaurants, and to see the sights.

One day during a spell of golden autumn weather Marie-Anne was taken with finding the source of the river Lot, which flows past our house, where it is about two hundred metres wide. Although it is only a tributary of the Garonne, the Lot is a longer river than the Thames. It is also very winding, proceeding in a succession of loops and in places through spectacular gorges; at La Canourgue the Lot is only about fifteen miles from the famous gorges of the Tarn.

The journey took us to the nice old town of Espalion, and on to Mende, the prefecture of the most thinly populated department in France, Lozère. From Mende we carried on to Bagnols-les-Bains, where the Lot is just a rippling stream. Bagnols is a delightful village-like spa, whose mineral springs were first discovered by the Romans, at ease in its valley between the forested slopes of the Massif Central. At the next village, Le Bleymard, at the foot of Mount Lozère, we asked directions to the source of the river.

'You are about five kilometres off,' we were told. We followed the main road further and then turned off into the hills until we found a signpost to the farm where the river actually began.

In the farmyard a man was tinkering with a car. In answer to Marie-Anne's question he took us round the back of a barn and halfway along the side of a field to a rock.

'Voilà!'

There was nothing there but dry and dusty earth. 'That's where it starts,' the man went on. 'That is in most years, it does. But this year, because of the drought, it starts down in the valley. About five kilometres from here.'

We looked at each other and at the man. In a voice which seemed to acknowledge both our disappointment and eccentricity, he said, 'If you really want to see it, go back to the main road towards Bleymard and keep your eyes open towards the left of the road. You should see a place where there is a small rocky pool. That's where it starts in dry years. Never further away than that.'

We thanked him and went back and found the pool, about a hundred and fifty metres from where we had asked the first man.

The river bubbled up from beneath a rock about two feet square, and beyond it the land rose up to the six thousand feet of Mount Lozère, which the locals call the bald mountain, because its slopes and summit are treeless.

Though the road had been gloriously picturesque, following its narrow windings beside the river all the way from Cahors had been time-consuming, so, mission accomplished, we made our way back to Mende, where we stayed the night in a small hotel.

When Marie-Anne was a schoolgirl, boarded permanently with nuns, because her father and step-mother were almost always in Africa, and because, in any case, her step-mother didn't like her, she used to be sent for a summer holiday to a little place called Binic, in Brittany, or to Arcachon on the Atlantic coast, where she was received 'en famille' by a sister of one of the nuns. When we married, we spent our honeymoon in this rather stylish old resort, and have always retained what I suppose is a sentimental attachment to it. It is only about two hours' drive from the house, so several times a year, usually outside the summer season, we drive there and have lunch in a seafood restaurant overlooking the Bassin d'Arcachon, the great land-locked bay, usually busy with graceful yachts and windsurfers, as well as the occasional sardine fishing boat. After lunch there is time for a walk on the huge sandy beach near the Dune de Pyla and a swim, before driving back through the forest in the evening light.

It's nice to think that we can go to lunch in Spain, and it's true. The river Garonne rises in Spain, as the Garona, and by following its valley through the Pyrenees, where it is a tumbling trout stream, you can cross into Spain by a road which involves very little mountain driving. You arrive at a small town called Vielha, which in winter is a popular base for winter sports enthusiasts, and where there is a parador with a cool terrace and views of the mountains. The parador has the usual beautifully furnished rooms and a restaurant where, especially on Sundays, they offer a magnificent lunch in true Spanish style, a complete change from our local French cuisine. Dishes often found on the menu include roast venison, a stew of marcassin (young wild boar), baked mountain trout with a red wine sauce, roast sucking pig, and a paella which is to the usual tourist version as Christmas cake is to bread and butter.

We make this trip about once a year. We can be sitting down to lunch in the parador three hours after leaving home. It's a comfortable drive along roads which are straight for long stretches and almost traffic free at any time of year, and which pass through pleasant scenery dotted with ancient villages and with the lovely range of the Pyrenees, dominated here by the ten-thousand-foot Pic d'Aneto, always straight ahead and becoming closer and bigger all the time. The route passes through the little town of Bossòst where the well-known attachment of the Pyreneans to smuggling remains alive in the duty-free shops, where Havana cigars, Scotch whisky and other luxury goods can be bought at remarkably low prices.

We once made this trip completely on impulse. It was a Saturday morning in July and it seemed that we had been sweltering for ever in the high nineties, and we looked at each other over breakfast and Marie-Anne said, 'Wouldn't it be nice to be in the mountains?'

So off we went, planning to stay just one night. I had enough money for petrol but little to spare and our local bank was closed on Saturday, but I had my Visa card to settle the hotel bill. At Vielha we registered in the parador, and then drove a few miles up into the mountains, where we found an isolated inn. The mountain air was cool and we ate lunch inside at a window table with stupendous views. In the evening we dined in the parador, though I don't remember what we had. All I remember is what happened on Sunday morning.

When we went down to pay our bill after breakfast, there was already a queue. A couple of people paid without undue delay, and then the lady in front of me took her turn. Time went by. Physically, she seemed timid, a middle-aged thin, spinsterish, rather nun-like person, but she was not too timid to query her bill. She went through it item by item, requiring everything to be explained to her, and apparently checking the spelling of every word, and commenting on the cost and value of each item, oblivious to the lengthening queue behind her. The Spanish cashier did his best in halting French to help her along. 'Yes, the dinner was good value.' No, he regretted, but that particular service could not be offered any cheaper. And so on.

The French are not noted for their patience and I could hear mutterings from the back of the queue. But the man behind me was English. 'Long-winded old so-and-so,' he said not very gallantly, but accurately expressing the current public opinion.

'It's a wonder,' I said to him conversationally, 'how some people manage to get through everyday life, making such a meal of simple things.'

'Ain't it just,' he said. He was a muscular, tough-looking middle-aged man in expensive sports clothes, who looked exactly what I later discovered him to be, a prosperous scrap metal dealer from south London, a man accustomed to take the short way through trouble, and who would certainly have known one Kray brother from another.

The nun-like lady departed, well satisifed. My turn. I passed over my Visa card. The Spaniard took it away, and came back with a face that said clearly, 'This is going to be one of those mornings,' but despite the fact that his patience must have been already severely tried, he spoke with the usual Spanish courtesy. 'I am sorry, sir, the machine refuses your card.'

I said what everybody says. 'There must be some mistake. Please check.' He did. There was no mistake, the card could not be used. I was, as they say, non-plussed. I knew I had sent a cheque some days before, but on reflection I also knew that letters from south-west France could sometimes take almost a week to reach destinations in England outside London.

'What's up?' said the man behind.

'They won't take my Visa card,' I said. 'I don't know why.'

'I've got my cheque book,' said Marie-Anne. 'I'll give you a cheque.'

The cashier regretted with infinite politeness that he was not authorised to accept a cheque in French francs.

'We do not have enough money with us to pay in cash.' The Spaniard shrugged ever so slightly. That, he seemed to suggest, was regrettable.

'We shall just have to stay another night and sort it out when the banks open tomorrow morning,' I said.

Don't worry, friend,' said the man behind me. 'I'll look after this.' He said nothing about how some people managed to get through life without being able to cope with a simple credit card. He just moved in front of us, offered a gold card to the cashier, and in a quiet voice which was nearer an order than a request, said, 'Charge this gentleman's bill to my account.'

And so it was. He completely ignored our insistent refusals, as well as his wife's raised eyebrows. She said nothing, knowing that she, too, would be ignored.

We exchanged addresses, and Marie-Anne and I drove home very much impressed. I have always considered myself reasonably generous and easy-going but I could not help wondering whether, if the positions had been reversed, I would have done the same. On the whole I doubt it.

Two days after we returned home I received a letter from Barclaycard instructing me not to use my card until I had sent the payment, which in fact I had sent ten days previously. In the mean time I had sent a cheque to the Good Samaritan and invited him to come and stay with us, whenever he was in this part of France. He wrote to thank me for the cheque and the invitation but we have not heard from him again. On the journeys we have made since that incident I have been careful to make sure that there would be no problems over credit cards.

As well as motoring for pleasure we use the car a great deal in the local fashion. We do all our shopping by car – the nearest shop is two miles away. We visit friends by car. We fetch family and children from the airport (seventy miles distant) or the station (twenty miles distant) by car. As Marie-Anne prefers to be a passenger, I do all the driving, and enjoy it, but with all the mileage we do it is, perhaps, not surprising that I have had the occasional brush with the gendarmes. Unless he can actually see a police car or police motorcyclists, the average French driver is almost always exceeding the speed limit, as anyone who has driven down an autoroute at 130 k.p.h. well knows, and I do not claim to be an exception. I have been stopped and fined for speeding three times. It's quite painless, if you remain polite and say as little as possible, and it can throw an interesting light on French bureaucracy. On the last occasion I was summoned to court but, on the mayor's advice, wrote an apologetic letter regretting my forced absence on business on the date of the hearing. The penalty was a fine, which had to be paid promptly, and the suspension of my licence for one week.

The offence was on 8th August. Time went by and nothing happened about my licence. I went on driving. It was soon well into September and I had a week or two of research to do in Brittany. Not knowing what my position was I again sought the advice of the mayor of my commune.

'Have you paid the fine?' he asked. Money almost always comes first in French thoughts.

'Yes.'

'Good. Well, off you go, then. Until the police take your licence, it's yours. They are busy. They may forget. They may never come.'

I took him at his word, but returned from Brittany ten days later expecting to find a peremptory summons to the local gendarmerie. Nothing. Then again for a long time, nothing.

It was Boxing Day (not a holiday in France) when at last they telephoned and asked me to bring my licence in and leave it with them. No, they didn't mind if I took my wife shopping first. After all, said the gendarme, one must eat.

Chapter Ten

ANYONE FOR SNAILS?

In this part of France and, I suspect, most other areas, the chief topics of conversation are food and money. Sport is a good runner-up, but politics and the weather are non-starters, and sex is a preoccupation rather than a subject for conversation.

No, food is the common ground. The French, both men and women, are energetic in their pursuit and judgement of food and wine, and are ready to defend and promote their favourite recipes and vintages at any time.

But all this enthusiasm is historically recent. It is a mistake to think that French cuisine was always marvellous or, indeed, that it is always marvellous. In the past travellers to France had a low opinion of the standards of food and accommodation offered. When Dr Charles Burney, a friend of Dr Samuel Johnson, visited Aix-les-Bains in 1773, he wrote, 'Nothing can have a more antique and ruinous appearance than the whole town which, however, is in summer a good deal frequented on account of its waters, in despite of every inconvenience of bad lodging, provisions, etc.' Similar opinions were still being expressed in the late nineteenth century and even those who visited France in the 1950s frequently complained of the poverty and monotony of French hotel menus, of the inadequate sanitation, uncarpeted floors, naked light bulbs and general discomfort.

All that has changed. The enormous improvement in hotel and restaurant meals over the past fifty years stems from the enterprise and skills of a few great chefs, who realised that the spread of international business, plus tourism for everybody, would greatly increase the rewards of running good hotels and restaurants. Nowadays one cannot write about any part of France without mentioning food, and Gascony is no exception. The French public has become discerning in matters of restaurant meals, and their insistence on value for money and their readiness to complain the moment things are not right have kept standards high. They are constantly on the alert for any place that offers a good meal, and indeed any raw material which may offer a good meal. I'm sure that if some exotic but edible animal should stray into the wilds of Gascony, a kangaroo or a buffalo, for example, its chances of avoiding conversion into grilled steaks or a casserole with red wine would be strictly limited.

In the countryside of France cooking is done by electricity, which is available everywhere, or on wood-fired ranges, which some farmers' wives still prefer for certain dishes. But serious cooks follow the example of France's greatest living chef, Paul Bocuse, who refuses to cook by electricity, which he finds harsh and inflexible, and cook with gas. Outside the towns, and often inside them, this means bottled gas. There are depots for gas bottles in garages and grocers everywhere. Small bottles are collected by car, but the large cylinders, about five feet tall, are usually delivered and changed by a man from a depot.

The average Frenchman is constantly on the alert in matters of food, and remains faithful to the dishes of the past, when times were not so good. Our gas man is just such a Frenchman. Our gas bottles are kept against the wall of what M. Rambaud called the 'chauffeur's room' behind lavender and rosemary bushes at the back of a flowerbed. When one has to be renewed, the gas man comes in a decrepit Citroën van and launches into a struggle at close quarters with a cylindrical gas bottle a little taller than he is. He looks as if he is no match for it, being apparently frail and slightly bent and having been on the verge of retirement ever since we have known him, but so far he has always won. First of all he manhandles it on to a trolley cradle which he never fails to tell me he designed himself and means to patent one day. He then wheels it to the edge of the lavender bed, wraps his arms around it, gets a firm grip and, as if he were rushing Marilyn Monroe across the room to a Turkish divan, sweeps it into position. But on one occasion, just as he lifted it from the trolley, he stopped suddenly, apparently transfixed. Oh, Lord, I thought, he's slipped a disc.

Now what? I'll have to get the doctor – how do you say in French, 'The gas man has slipped a disc'? But instead of a groan of agony, he gave a gentle gasp, something between reverence and ecstasy.

'Ah, I see you have snails,' he said. 'Do you mind if I look around?'

Half an hour later he came to report that the job, which normally took him about five minutes, was done, and that he had found sixteen snails. Together with those he had found the day before, he had more than thirty, a veritable feast.

'These are the Bordeaux Petit Gris,' he told us, 'the finest, tenderest snail you can get, far superior to your Burgundy snail.'

'Will you have them for lunch?' I asked.

'Not this week,' he said. 'Snails take the flavour of whatever they have been eating. It might have been a plant with a bitter leaf. You have to feed them on something good for a week, so that they take on a fine flavour. Some people feed them on flour, or barley. But I keep mine in a dish of vermicelli. It's a matter of personal taste. It took me a few years of experiment to find out, but I can tell you nothing beats vermicelli. In a week's time they will be delicious, oh, delicious.'

I remain, and am likely to remain, unconvinced, though Marie-Anne enjoys a good dish of snails.

Another example of this alertness over food occurred when our little ornamental pond, normally the peaceful home of some very quiet goldfish, was invaded by a bullfrog and his mate, who thought they had found a bijou residence, away from all those rough types in Mme Lambert's little lake across the field. It might have been so, but unfortunately the garden pond is quite close, as the croak carries, to the bedroom in the pigeonnier, and guests complained that the frogs' nightly revels kept them awake. It is a lot harder to catch a frog in water than it might seem. It can be done in the clear waters of a swimming pool but even there it requires patience and ingenuity, since any fit frog can swim faster than a net can be moved against the resistance of the water. Catching one in a muddy pond where there are hiding places beneath water-lilies and stones is an impossibility.

I mentioned the problem to M. Zagillioni who occasionally does odd jobs for me, and happened to be spreading fresh gravel on the paths. He was one of those men who usually had a better idea than yours about how to do anything, and was sometimes right. According to him the way to catch a frog was with a fishing rod baited with a piece of bright red wool. They couldn't resist it, he said, especially on a cloudy day. This was a bit too much for me, and I tried to think of the French for 'Pull the other one', but idioms are always difficult and I had to be content with a lame 'C'est pas vrai'. He insisted that he was serious. Somehow I could not see myself making a success of this, and said so.

'Then you'll have to kill them,' he said. 'If you take them out, they'll just come back. Not easy to kill a frog. I'll tell Pierre about it at lunchtime. He'll know how to deal with it.'

Pierre was his cousin, and, as it happened, the mason who was working on the restoration of our second cottage, the fermette. He is a kind of genial Hercules, always pleasant and good-natured and capable beyond the ordinary. He lives not far from us, and that same evening he drove up in his van, after work and before supper. By sheer chance the frogs were sitting a few feet apart on the stone edge of the pool. I was interested to see what Pierre would do. It was all over in no time. He emerged smoothly from his van with an air rifle in his hand, spotted the frogs at once, and one-two, plop-plop, and that was two dead frogs.

'Well, thanks, Pierre,' I said, not knowing what else to say.

'Do you want them?'

'Er, no.'

'Because they are very good to eat, and if you don't want them, I'll take them home for supper.' He fished them out, put them in his hat on the seat beside him, and drove off.

Unlike snails, which I want nothing to do with, I used to find frogs' legs quite acceptable, though I would not say, as some do, that they taste like chicken. But there is a difference between tolerance and enthusiasm, and I certainly could not imagine Marie-Anne dissecting frogs and frying the legs. To tell the truth I don't think I have eaten any since that evening.

As the gas man said, it's all a matter of habit and personal taste. I remember Marie-Anne's father, who in his youth was a professional big game hunter, telling us that a python cutlet grilled

over a wood fire was a dish fit for kings, and that certain
caterpillars grilled were very like scampi, if not better.

M. Zagillioni's information on what some countrymen will and
do eat was hardly less surprising. 'It's not only gypsies who eat
hedgehogs,' he told me once. 'I have not tried them myself but I
believe they are very good, though not as good as roast squirrel.
That's a more refined dish. They live on nuts, the flesh is clean.
Fox is not so good, though some say it makes a passable stew. I
suppose you can eat almost any animal, it's all a matter of the way
you prepare it.'

Then there is the local character known as M. Ragondin. Not
his real name, it is in fact the French for 'coypu'. This large aquatic
rodent of the beaver family is not uncommon on the banks of the
Lot, and some people, and M. Ragondin in particular, consider
that it makes a very good dinner, baked, I believe, as the gypsies
are said to cook hedgehogs, wrapped in clay. Anyway, when
riverside dwellers in this region want to be rid of coypus, they call
in M. Ragondin.

Snails, frogs and songbirds (it is still possible to buy thrush pâté
in this part of France) found their way into the local diet at a time
when farmers had to be self-sufficient and men who worked long
hours in the fields had to do it on an average of 1700 calories a
day, hardly half of what they needed; anything extra that was
edible was welcome. The farm workers eat much better today, but
the habits formed then have persisted. After any summer shower
people with baskets can be seen searching the grass verges of the
roads outside the villages, looking for snails. Family menus are
also augmented occasionally when a hunter brings home something for the pot. In the south-west deer, wild boar, wild goat and
hares are among the animals hunted, with only occasional success,
as well as game birds. When you see chevreuil (wild goat) or lièvre
(hare) on a restaurant menu, they are rarely likely to be local
produce. The goat more often comes from Austria, and the hare
from Patagonia.

Restaurants today do make full use of the wonderful range of
local produce now available. Fresh fruit and vegetables in variety
rare in Britain (in the local market on any one day there could
well be six kinds of onion, five kinds of mushroom and four kinds

of turnip) are augmented by superb lamb from the hills of Quercy, Charollais beef, corn-fed chickens, geese, ducks and game birds of all kinds. A great deal of the fresh food in the local hypermarket is produced within a few miles of where it is sold.

I was introduced to the richness of the south-west in this respect some years before coming to live here. During a car tour of the region with three friends, we stopped for lunch at a small fishing inn on the banks of the Dordogne, not far from the lovely village of La Roque-Gageac. It was out of season, a fitful day changing between showers and sunshine, and we did not expect much. The landlord apologised for not having a choice to offer, but said that he would do the best he could. He showed us into a dining room like that of a small private house – the inn had only four bedrooms – into which four tables had been crowded. It was typical of rural France, flowery wallpaper, faded family photographs, a long-case clock in the corner, stopped who knows when, a window with a view of the river and another looking out on to a flowery garden, a vegetable plot, the corner of a chicken run, and fields and woods beyond. There was no one else there. With a bottle of wine to encourage us, we waited, and hoped, and wondered.

The meal began with vegetable soup, served in a huge tureen which was left on the table. It was so good that we all took two helpings in case there was nothing better to follow. There was, and plenty of it. First, an omelette, incredibly light and that deep golden colour that only fresh farm eggs can achieve, and gener- ously stuffed with chopped truffles. Next came a grilled trout served with a creamy sauce with a hint of tarragon. I for one was already well satisfied, but there was much more to come. We were in no hurry, and in the longish pauses between courses the landlord brought more bottles of a deep purple wine, and we watched a boy in a red canoe idling on one of the loveliest rivers in Europe.

After the trout came a dish of confit of goose, like that I was to be offered years later at Mme Lambert's lunch after the grape- picking. Next came lamb's tongue with capers, a masterpiece that melted in the mouth. Then the landlord insisted that we should try his wife's home-made goat cheese, and then her strawberry gâteau. It was a long-winded meal, and perhaps because of that, and the sensible portions, and the wife's superb cooking, the feast did not lie heavily on the stomach, and we went on our way happy and contented. The most surprising thing about this meal was neither its quality nor the quantity but that, as the landlord proudly told us, everything we had eaten, apart from the truffles, which came from a wood about three miles away, and the trout, which had been fished from the river outside his door, came from his own land, and his own livestock, and the wine from his own vineyard.

On this same trip we stopped at the Hôtel Madeleine in Sarlat for an evening meal and I remember that there again we had truffle omelettes, each of which must have contained a couple of ounces of truffles. For years now the black truffle of Périgord, 'tuber melanosporum', has become more and more rare, and at the same time the demand has steadily increased. In the past four years, when there have been successive droughts, the price has rocketed. In Monpazier, the mushroom 'capital' of the south-west, the true black Périgord truffles were selling one recent winter at the equivalent of £300 a kilo. At this price, it seems to me unlikely that the Hôtel Madeleine can offer truffle omelettes these days, certainly not like those of ten years ago, which, at current prices, must have had about £25 worth in each omelette. Even expensive restaurants rarely use truffles these days and when they do the price is exorbitant and you need a magnifying glass to find the black specks indicating their presence. I know just one restaurant in Cahors where, for about £30, you can have a small truffle tart.

The truffle is emperor, but there are many other edible mushrooms in the south-west and at least a dozen different varieties are available in the markets at various times of the year. The best of them, after the truffle, is called 'cèpe de Bordeaux', which costs a mere £10 a kilo. The field mushrooms, white on top and pinkish brown underneath, are called Paris mushrooms in France and, as in England, have a good flavour only when they grow wild and are freshly picked. When we first came to this house, M. Rambaud's philosophy of neglect had created near the north side of the swimming pool, next to a ditch and in the shade of thin undergrowth and trees, the perfect conditions for these mushrooms. Here, in a damp bed of dead leaves and rotted pine needles left undisturbed for years, they grew to monster proportions. The first time I came across one, I regarded it with deep suspicion. It certainly looked like a field mushroom, except that it was the size of a small side plate or a large saucer. But I plucked up courage and picked it. When I fried it, a delicious odour came from the pan. I cut a small piece and, telling Marie-Anne to call the doctor at once if I fell writhing to the floor, I tasted it.

'Don't be daft,' she said. 'Of course it's an ordinary mushroom.'

I did not remind her that the local papers have stories every year of people dying from eating unfamiliar mushrooms, and a mushroom of this size was certainly unfamiliar. But she was right. It was not only good, it was delicious. I had some memorable breakfasts based on one such mushroom and two rashers of bacon; but the trees and shrubs had to go when the swimming pool was put into operation, and the mushrooms also went. A swimming pool has to be in full sun, and the habitat of these monsters was destroyed. If we have a spell of damp, warm weather at the end of summer, we sometimes get a crop of field mushrooms in parts of the orchard and they taste good, though they never grow very large.

We also get another mushroom, one of the boletus family, called 'cèpes' in France. It is not, unfortunately, the delicious cèpe de Bordeaux. Not knowing what they were, when I first saw them I took one across to M. Lambert for identification. He knew three things about it: one, it was a kind of cèpe; two, it was not a cèpe de Bordeaux; three, it was good to eat, especially fried with chopped garlic and parsley. We tried them but were not enthusiastic, and as there were quite a lot, Marie-Anne suggested I should take some of them across to Mme Lambert. I took a sharp knife – M. Lambert had told me they should be cut, not pulled up – and gathered a basket full of these big, brown-topped mushrooms. They grow up to six inches across, with a white spongy underside and a thick white stalk.

My arrival in Mme Lambert's farmyard loaded with the mushrooms caused a mild sensation. A man who had just bought some of her wine and was about to drive off, got out of his car and came across to me.

'I'll have some. How much are you selling them for?'

'We've got too many,' I said to Mme Lambert. 'I thought you might like some.'

'They are really good,' she said, having a close look at them. 'Hmm. That one's a bit old but the others are lovely. Don't go, Georges,' she called out to her husband, who, having had lunch, was climbing on to his tractor to start the afternoon's work. 'Come and see.'

M. Lambert dutifully got down and came across the yard. 'They look good,' he said.

'We'll have them now,' said Mme Lambert, walking into the kitchen and reaching for a frying pan. 'Do you like aubergines?'

'Yes, I do.'

'Ginette,' she called for her daughter. 'Go and fetch two nice aubergines for Monsieur.' By the time Ginette returned, the cèpes were sliced and in the pan and starting to sizzle and M. Lambert was sitting at the kitchen table in anticipation. I accepted the two glossy, purple aubergines and wished them 'bon appetit'. I thought it was robbery, but M. and Mme Lambert obviously felt that it was a fair exchange.

There are perhaps not many restaurants left like that of the fishing inn, now a private house, beside the Dordogne. But it is still possible to make discoveries and have memorable meals in this part of France. The stars of haute cuisine may be few, but we have a sprinkling, and there is a galaxy of sound regional restaurants. Not so long ago Marie-Anne and I stopped for lunch at an auberge in the village of Cadouin in southern Dordogne, after visiting the Cistercian abbey there. For hundreds of years this abbey was a famous place of pilgrimage. Two years after it was founded in 1115 the bishop of Le Puy presented the abbot of Cadouin with a piece of cloth which was believed to have bound the head of Christ on the Cross. It was said to have been found at Antioch during the Crusades. Over the centuries countless pilgrims on the way to St James of Compostela stopped at Cadouin to kneel reverently before this holy relic, among them Eleanor of Aquitaine, Richard the Lionheart, St Louis and the Emperor Charles V. The pilgrimages continued until 1934, when the abbot of the day, perhaps unwisely, allowed experts to examine the cloth. They unhesitatingly declared it to be a piece of oriental

A local bastide on market day.

cloth of the twelfth century embroidered with Kufic inscriptions of that time. In other words it had been new when given to the abbey. The pilgrimages ceased but visitors still go to the abbey to see the beautiful cloister, a fine example of Flamboyant Gothic style.

And until the owner retired recently, pilgrimages of a different kind were still being made to the inn we stopped at, the Auberge du Périgord, which offered a lunch in the regional style of staggering proportions and at a bargain price. I remember that when the landlord brought the soup, he put an open bottle of red wine on the table. I made to pour some into a glass. He put his hand on my arm.

'Mais non, monsieur. That's just for the soup. I'll bring the good stuff in a minute.'

This custom of pouring red wine into the soup is called 'faire chabrol', and is traditional in Gascony, but, apart from this inn in Cadouin, the only time I have actually seen it done was in Corsica about twenty years ago. I was eating a solitary dinner in the mildewed dining room of an ancient inn in the mountains in the centre of the island. There was no sound but the tick and creak of a grandfather clock which may well have been there in Napoleon's day, and the rheumy breathing of a bleary-eyed dog of great age and indeterminate race who was stretched on the flagstones in front of the empty grate. Suddenly the door was flung open and three men dressed in long black cloaks and wide-brimmed black hats, each carrying a rifle, clattered across the stone floor and sat down at the next table. The woman of the house, giving a fair imitation of a wine barrel in apron and slippers, followed them in and took their short order, which I guessed was the Corsican for 'the usual'. Having seen similar men in the fields, I supposed they were mountain shepherds. They launched into animated conversation which was not interrupted when the woman returned with a great bowl of soup, and then a huge loaf of bread and a litre of red wine. They helped themselves to soup, poured in some red wine, broke bread into it and stirred it round, and started on their supper. The conversation steadily became more heated and angry, and the man nearest to me had his hand on his gun, and looked ready to despatch his adversary on the spot. I thought of making a dash for the door, but curiosity or indecision kept me seated. Then, to my amazement, instead of picking up the gun, he burst into song. When he stopped another one had a go, and then the third, and so on. Within a short time, the tension had gone and they were laughing and joking with each other, and called for another bottle to lace what remained of the soup.

When I mentioned this incident to a Corsican writer, he told me that the custom of insulting people in impromptu songs was a traditional Corsican method of smoothing over arguments instead of coming to blows. It originated, he said, in the Roman legions when officers discovered that it is impossible to take seriously insults which are sung instead of shouted, and gave orders that disputes among the ranks should be settled in this way. I simply don't know if this is true, though it does sound possible. I admit that, apart from waiters in the few Italian restaurants, I have never heard anyone burst into song, insulting or otherwise, in a restaurant in Gascony.

Such is the fickleness of human nature that we find we miss Indian and Chinese restaurants which are either non-existent or indifferent in Gascony, though we went to them only rarely in London. Another thing we miss is fish and chips which we enjoyed occasionally and which is unobtainable here. Such things are subjective. Different people miss different things. One English friend resident here has been heard to say that he always looks forward to going home, because he'll be able to get a 'decent slice of bread'. I remember chatting to one English couple who visited us. It was late morning beside the pool.

'Soon be lunchtime,' he said, with some anticipation, I thought.

'Going out?' I asked, wondering which restaurant they had chosen.

'Oh, lord, no. We never eat French food. I'm a sausage and mash man, myself. Or bacon and eggs. Myrtle's favourite is shepherd's pie.' There was no answer to that.

Other people eat out on every possible occasion, and some keep notes of the restaurants they visit. Some come armed with Gault et Millau, or Champerard, or Bottin. There are other restaurant guides but these are the big three, and when they agree on the merits of a place, there's little doubt that it will be good. Michelin is good but much less detailed in its information.

Most of the restaurants in the region are sound or very good, but it is possible sometimes to go wrong. I remember one where the woman who came to take our order was so sloshed she had difficulty making her way between the tables.

Speaking slowly and carefully she said, 'I can recommend the trout. We have our own breeding tanks. We have our own bree . . . my husband will catch one for you.' We agreed and we watched her weave back to the kitchen.

'If he's as sozzled as she is, he'll never do it,' said Marie-Anne. He did, but it was poorly prepared. However, I remember it less for the rotten meal than the conversation at the next table, which Marie-Anne reported to me. We thought at first that a nice young man was taking his elderly mother out to lunch, but eventually deduced that he was a taxi-driver who had been taking his passenger to visit the local cemetery. Sickness and death are never far from the French mind. All Saints' Day is one of the milestones of the French year, when the entire French population seems to be on the move, returning to their natal villages to put flowers (chrysanthemums only) on the family tombs. It is also the day when more people are killed in road accidents than any other.

The Gascons regularly ask if you and your family are well, and they do it in a manner which suggests that they expect the worst and will be disappointed if they don't get it. Mme Lambert is a great one for this, and I have often been tempted to answer, 'Oh, we're fine, except that I've had a couple of fits lately and Marie-Anne has gout,' but she might take me seriously. Most Gascons wouldn't, they don't mind a morbid joke. Last time I asked the gas man how he felt, he replied, 'I'm ill, I ache all over, I'm getting old, but I'm not going just yet. Flowers are too expensive. I'll wait a few years.'

But to return to the restaurant conversation. It was not All Saints' Day. It was midsummer. The woman was clearly dissatisfied with the cemetery, and made a long complaint about it, and was politely supported by the driver. She finished by saying, 'I tell you what, that tomb next to mine is a disgrace. You know what they do, they clean it once a year for All Saints' and then they don't touch it again until the next year. Those Durands were always a scruffy, feckless crowd. I shan't be happy next to them, I can tell you that for sure.' From the vigour with which she held forth on the subject it seemed it might be some time before she actually took up residence.

It is typical of the Gascon farmer that he does not see why he should pay for a meal in a restaurant, when he can have the same thing as good, if not better, at home. The local people rarely eat out, except for the occasional Sunday lunch as a family celebration.

It was also typical of M. Rambaud, except that after his divorce, he preferred to eat in someone else's home. It's not easily done in these parts, but M. Rambaud was ingenious. He turned his sights on the nearest target, the Lamberts. If death is never very far from the French mind, the question of inheritance is even closer. M. Rambaud's ploy was to harp on the fact that he was getting on in years, in dodgy health and, above all, alone in the world. He told them how fond he was of Ginette, their only child. He thought of her almost as a daughter, he said, and somehow managed to persuade them, without actually putting anything in writing, that he would make her his heir. It was M. Caumont who told me this. 'He was always going there for Sunday lunch to talk things over,' he said, dryly.

If so many people always eat at home, how do the restaurants survive? Not all of them do; about a quarter of all the new ones that open, close within a year. Those that survive depend largely on businessmen, travelling salesmen, occasional functions, tourists and visitors from other parts of France. Happily, there are enough of these survivors to ensure that eating out in France remains an interesting and inexpensive pleasure.

There is, however, one thing almost entirely missing. Nobody gives dinner parties. Social customs are very different here from what they are at home. It is a popular saying that 'an Englishman's home is his castle', but I can tell you from experience and inquiry that, to a much greater extent, 'the Frenchman's home is his château'. The ordinary Frenchman, at least in this part of France, simply does not invite anyone apart from close relatives into his house. The idea of having a few friends round for drinks simply does not occur to him, and inviting someone to dinner just out of friendship is more or less out of the question.

The only occasional exception is the entertaining of an important business connection with a particular purpose in view, and even that is rare outside the cities. It is true that a near neighbour did invite us to dinner soon after we arrived and introduced us to several other couples, all of them with their own businesses and plenty of money. He is a successful accountant with his own aeroplane, sailing boat, Mediterranean house, and a finger in all kinds of property pies. It was at the time when the rumour was still current that we had more money than we knew what to do with, and he did put up a number of tentative business propositions. But, perhaps because he is so very busy, or had decided that after all we were not rich, which is true, or that if we were, we did not intend to invest locally, which would be true if we did have any money to spare, the invitation has not been repeated.

But in those days, new to French provincial life, we took the invitation at face value and duly asked them back, and as Mme Rambaud had called to see us, we felt we should also invite her and her new companion. On the day in question a plumber was fitting a more powerful electric pump and a new filter to our water supply which comes from a well in the orchard. In true plumbing tradition he had forgotten an essential something or other and had to tour the ironmongers in the local town to find it. In the mean time we had no water, and the time for preparing the dinner got closer and closer. Still no water, still no plumber. Marie-Anne began to show signs of stress of the why did I ask them? what shall I give them? perhaps they will forget or get lost? variety. Mme Rambaud might well get lost, I thought, but as her friend was a surveyor and the accountant lived only a few hundred metres away, it seemed unlikely that they would fail to arrive.

But everything was all right in the end. The plumber returned and got things working in the nick of time, and Mme Rambaud was late, having been delayed at the preview of an art exhibition in a neighbouring town. By the time drinks had been served and Mme Rambaud had told us how nice it was to be back in her house and which parts of the property were likely to fall down, Marie-Anne, who is a superb cook, had performed her magic in the kitchen. The pièce de résistance was a good old English steak and kidney pie. For some reason unknown, French housewives do not make pies, and it was, therefore, an unfamiliar dish. They do make open tarts, but we could not bring ourselves to offer a steak and kidney tart. The French, especially in the provinces, are very conservative; the pie was tackled with considerable circumspection and, when Marie-Anne explained that it was a traditional British dish, with barely disguised suspicion. However, the men soon succumbed to the delicious odours rising from their plates, and gladly took second helpings. Not so Mme Rambaud, who had clearly never seen anything like it before. She picked delicately at a couple of pieces of kidney, out of politeness, risked a little potato and gave up. We discovered soon after, when Mme Rambaud asked us to dinner, with the accountant and his wife, that this lack of enthusiasm was not be taken as a criticism.

Mme Rambaud had been brought up in a household in which all the work was done by servants, and had never cooked a meal in her life. The dinner was prepared by her companion, Henri. After what he called 'a country soup', which Marie-Anne later said was from a tin, served in an old-fashioned tureen, he brought in a very good looking roast joint surrounded by halved peaches. When he started to carve it, Mme Rambaud felt that as hostess, she ought to comment.

'Your roast pork is too pink, Henri,' she said. 'It's underdone. One can never be too careful with pork,' she said to the table at large.

Henri paused with the carving knife in the air, and with a friendly smile around the table and in a tone that was nearer to despair than exasperation, said, 'In the first place, this particular piece of pork happens to be veal. In the second place, if you roast veal too long, it becomes tough.' He continued placidly with his carving, and Marie-Anne kindly asked Mme Rambaud whether the impressive painting which dominated one wall was her own work.

'It's a copy I made of Corot's view of Florence from the Boboli Gardens. The original is in the Louvre. I did it to fill that space, the original is only about one third that size,' said Mme Rambaud, happy on her own ground.

Henri told us later that Mme Rambaud had no interest in food, often forgot about meals altogether, and, when she did eat, often did not know what she was eating and rarely asked. It was difficult to tell whether Mme Rambaud had constructed an artistic temperament to go with her profession, or whether it was genuine. The big argument in favour of her general vagueness was that it was her money which had paid for the house we had bought from M. Rambaud, and yet he was the one who owned it in the end.

No doubt Mme Rambaud, brought up in the ways of Parisian society, had returned our invitation out of courtesy, but she was not going to waste the occasion. After dinner we were taken round her studio and were shown many of her paintings.

'I'm preparing another exhibition of my work,' she said, 'but, of course, as you are friends, I would be happy to sell you anything you like beforehand, and then I'll just put it in as "sold".' Mme Rambaud's pictures were heavy with an obscure symbolism and also contained a lot of naked people who appeared to be made of something other than flesh. The accountant did his best to encourage me with occasional racy comments – 'Just look at those buttocks' – but I could do no more than make the occasional polite remark, and the truth was that I preferred her copies to her own original work.

In her total lack of interest in food Mme Rambaud was the exception that proves the rule. There are still many women in the region who take a great pride in their cooking ability, and in many of the local villages there are 'farm markets' on Sunday morning where the farmers' wives and other housewives sell their own home-made cheeses, jams, honey, bread, confits of goose, duck and pork, gâteaux of all kinds, splendid fruit tarts in season, and the feather-light tourtières, which are tarts made from pastry rolled so thin that its local name is 'wedding veil pastry', and filled with prunes or apples and laced with Armagnac brandy.

A great many housewives still can or bottle their own fruits and vegetables of all kinds, as well as various confits. If you should want to confound an English ironmonger, you could walk into his shop with a tray full of open cans of peas and ask him to seal them. It happens all the time here. In many ironmongers you will see a notice with the one word 'sertissage'. This is the service by which they sell the housewives the tins for their beans, tomatoes, etc. and guarantee to solder the lid on, when they bring them back full. There is still one man in the town who makes his living doing this, a 'sertisseur', who has a little, glass-fronted shop near the market. You can see him at work sealing and labelling the tins for his customers.

Regional home cooking reaches its peak in what are called 'fermes-auberges' – farm inns. These are working farms which offer holiday accommodation, usually only a few rooms, and where in the summer the farmer's wife opens a restaurant and offers the traditional regional dishes. The ferme-auberge must comply with certain government requirements, one of which is that the food offered must as far as possible be based on the best produce of the farm. As a rule they are open only in the high season, and for a few weekends and public holidays in early and late summer. In fine weather the tables are often arranged outside in the garden of the farm. They are all known for their copious helpings, and it is as well to be hungry when you arrive.

Between the fermes-auberges and the famous establishments with their Michelin rosettes, there are restaurants of all kinds and sizes. Tucked away in the provinces we may be, but we are never short of somewhere to go for a meal, except that it is not likely to be in the house of a French friend.

Chapter Eleven

SEX IN THE SUNNY SOUTH

It did not take us long to realise, after coming here, that there is a steamy side to life in the deep south. Whether it is the warm climate or the hot temperament of a southern and essentially Latin people, sex is ever present and the local villages throb with dramas between husbands and mistresses and wives and lovers. It is a rare issue of the local provincial paper which does not contain at least one news item of this kind. A jealous husband shoots his wife and then himself, a workman thinks his concubine was too friendly towards another man in a bar and in a drunken frenzy beats her to death on the way home, a lonely café in the forest is found to be packed to the eaves with girls willing to console passing lorry drivers and salesmen. Rivals for the affections of a lady nightclub owner come to blows in the club and cause a fracas which wrecks the place. The 'Madame' of a local 'maison' has a row with a rugby team celebrating an important victory, and is closed down by the police. Stories of this kind represent the eruptions of a sexual volcano which apparently simmers continually all through the south. We even have a local town called Condom.

I have mentioned all this to M. Caumont and other local friends, and the normal reaction amounts to a shrug of the shoulders and 'After all, we are people of the south. We are Latin and hot-blooded, like the Spanish, the Italians, the Corsicans, the Sicilians. Violence and revenge are in our blood.' The fact is recognised in French law, where 'crime passionnel' is a specific legal term referring to a murder committed in circumstances which produced an act of passion, and such crimes are much less severely punished than other murders.

The curious thing is that the background to all this extreme behaviour is a society which is both very formal and cautious. In the past in the farming community in this area most marriages were arranged. Two farmers might meet after Mass on Sunday, and one would say, 'What do you think about marrying your daughter to my son?'

'It's true, I have thought about it. But if I give you my daughter, what will you give me?'

A long period of bargaining would follow in what was essentially a business transaction relating to the land. Sometimes the local curé would be the negotiator. This custom has died out, the locals say, so no doubt it is just a coincidence that M. Caumont's son married the daughter of a neighbouring farmer, and that similar matches are by no means uncommon.

The curé no longer plays a part in negotiations, if there are any. These days the young people sort themselves out and tell their parents what they plan. Older people turn, not to the curé, but to what are called in France 'matrimonial agencies', never 'marriage bureaux'.

These businesses do not set their sights any higher than 'promoting serious unions'. No licence is required to run an agency of this kind, and there seems to be no fixed scale of charges. The usual claim is that they do not accept any client who is not legally free to marry, and to establish this they insist on seeing the identity card which everyone in France must carry, and the document called the 'fiche d'état civil' which shows whether the person is married, divorced, widowed or single.

'The majority of people who come to us are seriously seeking to marry or remarry, or at least to find a companion and a lasting relationship,' says one agent. 'They have usually been on their own for a time and have not succeeded in interesting anyone, so they decide to try us.'

The agency claims a success rate of 40 to 50 per cent, though matching people is by no means always easy. Women are especially difficult says this agent. They often set their sights far too high. 'The widow of a sergeant will come to us and say that, as she is used to the military life, she would be happy with a major or a colonel, or a waitress about five feet tall with not much of a figure and little education wants a cultured, good-looking man not less than six feet with green eyes and curly hair.' Another thing about women, she says, is that they are more materially minded, and the older they are the more materially minded they become. Men, apparently, are more romantic.

From the point of view of social climate, the interesting thing is that these agencies abound. They are not confined to a few large towns. Every small town in south-west France has three or four of them which are fairly respectable, and several others which are less so. Judging from our local give-away paper, which contains nothing but advertisements, there are large numbers of people of both sexes constantly on the lookout for sexual partners. About half of the announcements are from agencies trying to find partners for ageing widows and widowers, divorced people, timid men, unwilling spinsters and unmarried mothers. The language used in the ads varies between the private insertions and those from the agencies, but both have their own code and a lot of reading between the lines has to be done. Agency advertisements may have as many as twenty men and twenty women, with no more than a one-line description each. 'Renee, 59, saleslady, in the hope of your profound tenderness, Monsieur.' 'Pascale, 26, unmarried, a perfume of vanilla and cinnamon' seems mysterious at first, but turns out to be a convention for describing a coloured girl, many of whom come from the French Caribbean islands and Réunion, seeking husbands in France.

There are as many, if not more, advertisements inserted privately, some by people seriously hoping for marriage, and others of a different kind, no holds barred. They often show enterprise and make interesting reading. 'You, young girl or mature woman, alone and wanting affection, I offer you my services. I am 30, pleasant and virile.'

'Young girl, 29, very sexy and squeezable is looking for man of similar qualities.' This, says the agent, is more or less a prostitute looking for clients.

'Young man, 24, blond, blue eyes, seeks position with sympathetic masculine employer. Discretion assured.'

'Young married couple, fun-loving, seek young women for pleasant evenings and intimate games.'

In these privately inserted advertisements certain words recur repeatedly. An ad put in by a man which includes the word 'complicity' means that he wants sex, but expects to pay for it, in other words he is looking for a mistress. 'Pleasant outings and more if we suit each other' means a sexual relationship is the real object, but don't expect money and it would be appreciated if you paid your own share. 'Steady relationship' means sex on a regular basis, for its own sake and let's not waste time or money on anything else. Both men and women, 'married but reasonably free', seek partners for 'enjoyable afternoons'. And so on.

There are also numerous small display ads offering sexual services of every kind from professionals or willing amateurs – 'Meetings for Couples', 'The Network of Married Women', 'Muscular Love for Men', 'Between Men', 'Masterful Women' – as well as many advertisements from prostitutes, some of which have a sub-heading 'Erotically yours – every day except Sunday'. The approach is open and unrestricted; nothing seems to be banned. The paper is not pornographic, these pages are just there among all the others advertising unwanted furniture, lost pets, second-hand agricultural equipment, houses and employment. All these services, together with information on everyday subjects of all kinds, are available on Minitel, the video display unit supplied by the French post office.

What can be called the climate of sexuality is maintained in several other ways. Likely places for finding partners are numerous. For instance, every town, big or small, has several dancing clubs, nearly all of them 'retro', which means for old-time dancing, and expressly catering for an age bracket bound to include many divorced people. There are several of these clubs in our local town, which has a population of less than forty thousand, another one in a nearby town with a population about one eighth of that, and even one in our local village. There are nightclubs and discotheques scattered throughout the countryside, usually a mile or two outside the towns, where noise or rowdy behaviour bothers no one. In general they cater for a younger set than the dancing clubs, but there are also specialised clubs for gays, and for what are called 'partouzeurs', couples who seek other couples on a 'the more the merrier' basis. Others are a cross between nightclubs and film clubs, where pornographic films of all kinds can be seen. These have apparently suffered in recent years from the very rapid spread of shops which sell or rent video films and which have 'blue' films openly on display among crime thrillers and westerns. I'm told that, rather than go to a club, farmers who have had a hard week prefer to spend Sunday afternoon in bed with a film of their choice.

The beaches of the south-west have long been famous for their nudists. Originally there were beaches set apart for them, but a few years ago nudism became general everywhere on the Atlantic beaches, both among tourists and locals, to the extent that people in bathing costumes began to look out of place. This common rush to strip seems to have eased off, and we have noticed that, though there are still many topless women, complete nudity is much less usual than it was five or six years ago.

All this frankness about sex, and the apparently incessant search for new partners, may suggest that there is more extra-marital sexual activity in this part of France than there is in Britain or America. Whether this is ultimately true or not is anybody's guess. It certainly seems that relations between couples, whether married or not, go wrong more often or more dramatically. There have been seven 'crimes passionnels' in our county town in the past year, with three deaths. It is somehow difficult to imagine places in Britain of a similar size, like Cheltenham or Wigan, having a similarly explosive record.

About one marriage in three in the south-west of France ends in divorce – and a much higher percentage in the Paris area. According to a divorced friend of Marie-Anne, part of the trouble is that the famous Latin lover is often not up to his reputation.

'My ex-husband thought a lot of himself, because he could perform the sex act two or three times a night. But that is all he did, perform the sex act. It was always over in a few minutes, never any good for me. He had no interest in giving me pleasure, and no idea how to do it.' Her attitude is supported by recent research which shows that more than 50 per cent of French women consider their sex lives unsatisfactory, and would like more enjoyable sex and more of it. A recent opinion poll quoted on French television found that 30 per cent of French women, as against only 13 per cent of men, would like sex at least once a day.

The usual Gascon male is a good example of what modern feminists call a 'male chauvinist pig', very 'macho' and conscious of his dignity. It is said that a Gascon does not open his umbrella when it rains, so that it will last longer as a sign of distinction on public holidays. He believes strongly that women should keep to their own affairs, and leave him to his. Nevertheless, in most houses it is the women who rule the roost, but they are expected to do it discreetly, particularly on public occasions. If on leaving church the husband hesitates between turning left for the bar and right for home, the wife may give him a gentle prod in the right direction with the tip of her umbrella. If, nevertheless, he turns for the bar, she is likely to follow and order his drink.

There is still a strong feeling about what a woman's place is, and what she should do and not do. On the farm the wife was always, and still is, responsible for all the animals. 'Where there is a fat pig, there's a good wife,' is a Gascon saying.

Women used not to join the men or guests for meals, a custom which still exists in the Arab world and parts of Greece. She produced and served the meal, but stayed in the kitchen, nibbling a bit here and there while the others ate. Some say that this is a left-over from the long Moorish occupation of Spain and southern France, others that it was the woman's choice, that she preferred to supervise, to make sure everything went well.

In former times, not so long ago, the lesser rights of women were indicated in some curious ways. For example, iron fire dogs, on which the logs rest to give them air so that they burn steadily, come in pairs each of the same design. In the past one was taller than the other and was placed on the man's side of the fireplace, while the shorter one showed the wife's side. A genuine old pair like this is now a collector's item.

There is a Gascon saying that 'Marriage is a man's penitence, not his future.' A young man about to be married who confessed his sins to the priest before the ceremony was surprised that the priest imposed no penitence on him. 'You are about to be married,' he said, 'that's quite enough.'

The division of labour was even carried into religion. The holiness of the local priests was judged according to their success in chasing away storms likely to devastate the crops. The village priest of Lagarde had a particularly high reputation in this respect. One day when a storm threatened to ruin their harvest, some of the congregation called at the church to ask him to work his miracle. He was not there, so they asked the bell-ringer, who, greatly honoured, seized a statue of the Virgin and began to intone, 'Exsurge Domine . . .' At this moment the curé returned and asked, 'What on earth are you up to?'

'It's obvious, Monsieur le Curé. I'm chasing the storm away.'

'Idiot! You expect to turn aside a storm with the statue of the Virgin? Don't you know it's not women's work? Fetch me the statue of our good Lord Jesus.'

Of course, modern Gascons would scoff at this story. At least some of them would, but not for long, and not at all, if they were farmers.

That is the traditional past. Today there is undoubtedly a colourful and sometimes dramatic side to love and marriage in the sunny south but, entertaining as it is to those not involved, it should be seen against the background of a solid majority leading normal family lives. All the people we actually know in the neighbourhood have been married only once and for a long time. M. Rambaud was divorced it is true, but that was hardly surprising. It was his marriage which surprised people, not his divorce. The people who appear in the more colourful 'meetings' advertisements are really a small but significant minority, like the drivers who cause havoc on the French roads.

All the workmen who have done jobs for us have been solidly married, with the exception of a M. di Santo, a landscape gardener. He did not say whether he had ever been married, but when he worked for us he was still smarting from the fact that a concubine with whom he had lived for eleven years, and by whom he had a ten-year-old daughter, had left him without explanation to live with another man. M. di Santo was a serious, efficient, vigorous man in early middle age and what seemed to rankle most with him was that the other man was older.

'I'd got used to her,' he told me, 'but I wasn't sorry to see her go. She was always crying.'

The woman had left her daughter behind, and M. di Santo, who lived with his old parents, looked after her seriously, often leaving his work during the afternoon to fetch her from school. He very much wanted another 'companion' and had been to one of the agencies who had found him two 'possibles'. The first he met a few times but did not like. In his opinion she was untidy and did not seem to wash much. The second he got on with and liked a lot, but she had her own house and refused to leave it, and he felt he could not leave his aged parents. As far as I know, he is still looking.

Many couples live together without the formality of marriage. The official French term for this state is 'concubinage', though the modern tendency is to refer to companions – 'compagnes' – rather than concubines. Where the relationship is well established and common knowledge there may be tax advantages, and the woman is entitled to special consideration in the event of the sudden death of her companion, in an accident, for example.

The current 'anything goes' climate of casual relationships between the sexes is fairly new in this part of France. There was a good deal less tolerance in the recent past. Not so long ago there was a custom called 'chari-vari' which consisted in kicking up a row, banging on tins and saucepans, blowing trumpets and shouting insults, outside the home of people considered to be of bad character, which usually meant living in sin in the eyes of the Church. M. Caumont, who is sixty-four, remembers it occurring several times in his youth.

Sometimes the chari-vari would include a dummy, made of sacks and straw, of the guilty person mounted back to front on a donkey which was driven through the village, while the racket went on. Sometimes the ceremony was on a large scale, particularly when the victim was someone important. In a village called Beauregard, in the north of the department, a rich widower lived with a woman servant and had a child by her. The village spent weeks preparing a chari-vari which included a cavalcade of horses, a mock tribunal, mock lawyers, two men dressed to represent the guilty couple and most of the villagers, making a great deal of noise.

One farmer who lived with a woman worker and was repeatedly harassed by the chari-vari found his own solution. The next time the crowd arrived to pester him, he met them with a loaded shotgun, ordered them into the house and obliged them to sit in the kitchen at a long table loaded with cakes and wine, and commanded them to eat and drink as much as they wanted. They did so, and went home thinking that he was not such a bad chap, and left him alone afterwards.

The chari-vari seems to have died out now – the last one held locally was in 1950 – but other, more pleasant customs still survive. It was usual for a farmer to mark the birth of a daughter by planting a small wood of poplars. These trees take little more than twenty years to reach a marketable size, and when the daughter was to marry, the poplars were cut down to defray expenses and help with a dowry. This still happens occasionally.

There are customs associated with the marriage itself. One of these, which is very localised and does not occur south of the Garonne, is called 'la jonchée' – in English, 'the scattering'. On the day of the wedding the ground between the church and the Mairie where the bride will walk, and sometimes to the bride's house, if it is not far away, is scattered with greenery and a few flowers. One of the favourite plants used is box, which is said to bring happiness, and one which should never be used is laurel, said to bring bad luck. As part of the jonchée the gateway to the bride's house is decorated, often with two small pine trees, or bushes, adorned with ribbons and paper flowers. The decorations may be quite simple, just a few flowers along the garden fence, or much more lavish, and they are left in place until they weather away.

Another custom which is still quite common in the countryside is 'le tourain'. This is a soup made with stock, bread, eggs and garlic, and anyone who has eaten much in French country restaurants will have seen it on the menu. It is an everyday dish. But on wedding days it has a special role. In the peasant community the newly-weds do not as a rule leave after the wedding for an expensive honeymoon. Instead there is a wedding feast, then singing and dancing, after which they leave to spend the night together, usually in the house of a relation or friend. They often do not say where they will be, perhaps because they do not want to be disturbed by the 'tourain'. But somebody always knows where they are and customs must be followed, so at some time after midnight, a group of friends goes to the house and makes a great noise, singing and shouting, so that the couple know what to expect. Then the friends invade the bridal chamber, taking with them a tureen full of the 'tourain' which the young couple drink sitting up in bed. Traditionally, the idea is to symbolise a life of prosperity in which they will never want. Occasionally, the custom is repeated when a couple move to a new house, even after years of marriage, but in this case it is more of a house-warming, with music and dancing and then, towards midnight, 'tourain' is eaten in the company of friends in the dining room, not sitting up in bed.

The sounds of all this gaiety carried across the fields to us on the night when M. Caumont's son was married, but we were newcomers and had never heard of the 'tourain'. We just thought they were having a rather riotous party.

If the dancer from the Moulin Rouge represented an aspect of life which is still common in this part of France, the Caumonts are typical of more conventional country life. Sons, because they will eventually take over the farm, are considered especially important in farming communities, and when the birth of one is announced, someone is sure to say, 'Well, that's another pair of hands.' M. Caumont père, a practical man rather than a sentimentalist, did not conceal his pleasure when, following his son's marriage, two sons were born in quick succession, and then a daughter. He himself had had three daughters and only the one son, and had been afraid that his son might follow suit. Two of his three daughters also have three children, and often the nine of them are there together. The sound of their young voices raised in play wafts across the fields to us and their games can produce as much noise as there was on that wedding night.

Chapter Twelve

CAME THE WINTER

When we first arrived in Aquitaine and had time to look around we were very impressed by the variety and splendour of the trees and flowering shrubs, and the general lushness of the vegetation. Britain is famous for its lovely gardens, but here a well-ordered garden was then a rarity. On the other hand we saw everywhere plants which we had never seen, even in the south of England, and some which we did know, but only as sickly relations of what we found here. I had seen tamarisks, for instance, on the coast near where we lived in Sussex, but only stunted and bent by the wind and with a lot of bare twigs and no flowers. Here the tamarisk, bush or tree, has long, graceful branches, richly green, and covered in spring or summer (there are two kinds) in pink blossom. Almost every house with any land here had its own mimosa tree, heralding the spring in the first days of March with sheaves of musky perfumed golden blossom. Marie-Anne had always wanted one, and I think it was the first thing we planted. The 'garden', as M. Rambaud had left it, had around its 'informal' lawn several indicators of the local sub-tropical climate, two kinds of spiky, cactus-like agaves, yuccas, several palm trees, including two Canary Island palms, and a group of bananas.

In front of Mme Lambert's house there is a magnificent magnolia grandiflora taller than the house, and similar specimens are to be seen in all the local villages. On the south-east wall there was a thirty-year-old lemon tree which she said never had fewer than two hundred lemons on it. The lemon is a fascinating tree in that its whole life cycle goes on at the same time: it carries sweetly scented flowers, small young fruit, ripening fruit, young pale green leaves and dark glossy leaves simultaneously and all year round.

Lemon trees are usually grown in tubs and taken under cover during winter cold spells, but M. Lambert's was in the ground and grew to the eaves of the house, and in winter he just draped a plastic sheet over it. Big Judas trees, a mass of pinky-mauve blossom in early May, were to be seen everywhere. The bananas, usually in the corner of a sunny courtyard near the house, and often more than ten feet tall, really surprised us, and everywhere in June there were the red and pink blossoms of oleander bushes. Silk trees (albizzia) and sweetly scented catalpas were common, and many houses had a vine for table grapes around the porch, and somewhere nearby a fig tree loaded with juicy fruit every year.

Such winter as there normally is here, and it usually amounts to no more than occasional grey skies, some rain, and a few days of frost, usually holds off until January, and that was the pattern of our first winter. But the following year, on Boxing Day, the temperature fell sharply and our troubles began. They continued for weeks. As the days went by it became colder, then it snowed, then it froze harder, then it snowed again.

We had filled the swimming pool that summer. It had taken ten days, using two garden hoses, one from the well, and one from the spring under the barn. As it had taken so long, we decided to leave the water in it, and filter it from time to time during the winter. It froze over. Then the snow covered the ice, and this snow which, we believed, arrived once in ten years and lay on the ground for half an hour, decided to stay for weeks. It froze harder and snowed some more and the outline of the pool disappeared under a flat blanket of snow that covered the whole of the pool garden. Under the snow the ice on the pool was six inches thick – a troupe of circus elephants could have practised their act on it with impunity.

To begin with it was all rather picturesque, and had the charm of the unexpected, but it became colder day by day, and one morning we got up to find that none of our taps offered anything but splutter and hiss. Of water not a drop.

Investigation showed that the pump which raised the water from the well, filled the cistern and pumped the water to the kitchen, the bathrooms and loos, had burst. We called the plumber, not expecting him to arrive that day, since similar things were happening left, right and centre, but to our surprise he came within the hour. All he was doing, he said, was touring the district telling people there was nothing he could do.

'At this temperature' – it was by then below −15 degrees Centigrade – 'there is no point. It will just happen again. Not even insulation will keep this cold out. You would have to heat all the time, and there is no power point in the pump room.'

Even if there had been the result would have been problematical, since the local electricity authority seemed to be totally unprepared, and was already making prolonged power cuts.

'At least you are better off than some,' said the plumber, climbing back into his van, ready to tell someone else there was nothing he could do. 'You still have the hand pump under the barn. Rambaud told me once that in sixty years that has never frozen, nor run dry. Call me again, when the thaw comes.'

In the panic of having no water at all, we had forgotten for the moment what M. Rambaud had called the 'source'. This was a second well, at least it looked like a well, though not as deep as the big well in the orchard, but M. Rambaud called it a spring because, he said, it was fed, not by the water table of the river Lot like the big well, but from an underground spring which came down from the hills.

When we had first shown interest in buying the house, M. Rambaud had made a great to-do about this spring, citing it as one of the reasons he could not reduce his price.

'It's pure mineral water,' he said. 'The formula is almost the same as Contrexéville. You must have heard of Contrexéville, it is one of the most popular bottled waters in France. You are not just buying a house. You're buying a potential business. You can bottle and sell this water. The Americans were very impressed, it was what decided them, really.'

He had told us about the Americans before. A wealthy family with vineyards in California, who wanted a place handy for Bordeaux so that they could keep in touch with the French wine industry. Unhappily they had been killed in a plane crash, he said, actually on the way to sign the purchase papers.

'Where was that?' I asked.

He looked at me as if I were simple-minded. 'America,' he said.

I did not know what to say to this. I had been unable to believe in the existence of the family or the unfortunate plane crash when he first mentioned them, and slightly more experience of M. Rambaud and his fantasies did nothing to dispel my disbelief. On the other hand I was ready to believe that he might have created a fantasy American buyer, for whom he had invented the mineral water story, knowing that hygienically minded Americans would have been terrified of well water.

'Everybody round here has a well,' said Marie-Anne practically. 'They can't all go in for bottling mineral water.'

There's no answer to that, I thought. But M. Rambaud had an answer for everything. He glanced around furtively as if the barn was full of avid peasants trying to steal his secret, and dropped his voice.

'Madame, I've told you. This water is different. It has been analysed. I would have bottled it myself, but sadly I no longer have the capital. Wait, I'll show you.' He scuttled into the house and returned a few moments later with a thin file of documents.

'There, look at that,' he said. 'What do you make of that?' He showed me a document, headed 'Analyse Complète', made by a chemical institute in Narbonne some years previously. From the breakdown I could see that it was strong in calcium and bicarbonate of soda, and contained magnesium, iron, sulphur and other compounds, the proportions of which meant nothing to me. The institute's conclusion was that it was hard water, meeting all the requirements of good drinking water.

'It does seem to be drinking water,' I said cautiously.

'Rather more than just drinking water,' said M. Rambaud, in a hurt tone. He dived into the file again and with a flourish produced a letter.

'Ministry of Health. Paris,' he announced. 'Look here. Paragraph 2.' He read out, ' "According to the analyses carried out, this water would appear to have the characteristics of a mineral water." You see, I do not joke.'

He handed me the letter, which said exactly what he had claimed, and went on to explain what steps he would have to take to get authorisation to bottle and sell it. The only small doubt I had left was that, having avoided a pseudo-Stradivarius and a fake Ingres, I could not help thinking that just possibly M. Rambaud had helped his sample of water along a bit with a dash of Contrexéville or some other well-known bottled water. I don't know. The water certainly seemed pure and good to drink but not wanting a bottling plant on the premises, we have never had it analysed ourselves. The time may come, and disillusion with it.

Well, that was M. Rambaud's story of the water. Unfortunately, he had never had it piped to the house, so we had confined its use to watering the garden during summer droughts, so as not to lower the level in the well which did supply the house. So the spring water had to be pumped by hand, in the time-honoured medieval manner. We collected some buckets and I pumped them full. Enough water for the day. Things could be worse, we thought, and we were right.

The temperature fell a further five degrees overnight, and in the morning when I went to pump the water for the day, I found the pipes which had not frozen in sixty years, bulging and split with the ice inside visible. I took the cover off the well and dropped a small pebble down the shaft – splash! There was water there. It was just a question of raising it.

I could think of nothing more brilliant than a bucket on the end of a cord. Having lowered the bucket, which rested empty on the surface of the water, I laboriously wiggled it about until it took in water and sank. But, not having been a Boy Scout for long enough, there was something wrong with the knot I had used to tie the cord round the handle of the bucket, so that when I started to raise the full bucket it plopped back into the water and I was left with a length of cord in my hand and a bucket at the bottom of the well. I would have to fish for it. In a flash of inspiration I remembered seeing somewhere a large two-ended iron hook such as butchers use to hang sides of beef, and I suppose left over from the days when the farmer's wife had hung her own hams.

It took me some time to find it, and to tie it, this time securely, to the cord. The next thing I discovered is just how dark it is at the bottom of a well. Although the water surface was only about ten feet down, I could see neither the handle of the bucket nor the butcher's hook. Luckily, we had invested in a large and powerful electric torch. Unluckily, there was nowhere to rest it safely where the beam would reach the bottom. I did not want an electric torch as well as a bucket in the icy depths, so I called Marie-Anne, who came out in an old mink coat inherited from her step-mother and stood directing the beam of the torch down the well, while I knelt on the edge, to see better, and started fishing. I was wearing a pair of fur-lined boots which I had obtained on expenses for a winter trip to Moscow for the newspaper years before. I also had on a red fox-fur hat which I had brought back as a present for Marie-Anne. Despite the fact that anything she puts on her head looks stylish, and she looked ravishing in the fur hat, she has never worn it. I once gave her a dress length of beautiful yellow silk that I bought in Benares. It is still somewhere in the house in the depths of a trunk, untouched. It has always been like that. I won't let her choose me a tie or a shirt, and she won't wear anything I buy her on my own initiative.

As I leaned forward the hat slipped, but by some miracle I managed to save it from falling in, while teetering on the brink myself.

'Don't fall in,' screamed Marie-Anne.

It would have been a better story if I had done, but I didn't, and after ten minutes of patient, stealthy fishing, during which I kept telling myself that, if Eskimos could catch fish through holes cut in the ice, I could catch a more or less stationary bucket, I got it out. This time I made sure the knot was good and soon developed the knack of raising the full buckets without losing much of the contents.

It is not until you find yourself in a situation like this that you realise just how much water you use in a normal day. The water for washing, shaving and washing dishes had to be heated in an array of saucepans, and an important part of Marie-Anne's conversation seemed to consist of 'I need more water for washing up' or 'The bucket by the loo needs refilling.'

When I was not fetching water, I seemed to spend most of my time sawing and splitting logs for the fires needed to supplement the oil-fired central heating, which, as it required an electric spark to start, went off whenever there was a power cut, which was often.

'It can't last long,' Marie-Anne kept saying. But it did. With all the rough work I was doing, I began to feel somewhat dirty and in need of a bath. There is a small Logis de France in the village, a typical French country inn. After a few days without running water, it occurred to me to ask the landlady if she still had hot water. She and her husband were in the bar with a couple of their regular customers.

I put the question. She seemed rather surprised. 'But of course, Monsieur, there is hot water.'

'In that case would it be possible for me to come here and have a bath. I'd pay, of course, about ten francs, I suppose.'

The locals, who had already picked up my English accent, were fascinated and watched the exchange intently. 'He wants to pay for a bath,' one muttered to the other, with a broad grin. 'No, you must have it wrong,' said his friend, smiling even wider.

Madame's business sense was already alerted. 'With pleasure, Monsieur, but, you understand, the water has to be specially heated. It would have to be twenty francs. Let me show you the bathroom.'

I followed her, hearing behind me a voice saying, 'Did you hear that? Twenty francs for a bath!' and another, which I think was her husband's, 'He's mad.'

It was a good, big bath, and the thought of relaxing in it full of steaming, hot water was irresistible. I arranged to come back in an hour.

I don't know whether the word had gone round, but when I returned there were several more men in the bar. Apart from a muttered 'That's him' and 'He's an Englishman' my progress across to the stairs was watched in silence, but as I reached the landing conversation had broken out all round and there were hoots of laughter.

I made the most of the occasion. I filled the bath to the top, having poured in some foaming bath lotion, and luxuriated in it for a good fifteen minutes, then washed my hair and finished with a tepid shower. I dried myself, dressed, went down to the bar and paid across my twenty francs, watched in silence by the remaining drinkers.

'Everything all right?' asked Madame, with a smile.

'Very good. Thank you, Madame. I'll come back.'

But I had only one more bath there, because a couple of days after my second visit the temperature, having reached −23 degrees Centigrade, began to climb rapidly and the thaw set in.

In such small ways are reputations made. The story went round the village. I have been well known there ever since. I get friendly attention everywhere, and when we eat in the auberge, Madame comes to see us personally, tells us if there is something a bit special which is not on the printed menu, and stays for a chat. The garage man next door does minor repairs for nothing, and lends me extra bicycles for my visitors free of charge. Altogether I think it was a cheap bath.

The freeze, however, was far from cheap. As always in this situation, it was not until the ice melted and water began to come through the ceilings that we found out where the pipes had burst. In addition to the well pump, and the old pump under the barn, pipes had burst behind the kitchen sink, in the upstairs bathroom, and in the fermette but, worst of all, our installations in the newly finished pigeonnier were ruined before anyone had had a chance to use them. The brand new 200-litre hot water tank burst, despite its heavy insulation, and had to be replaced. There, too, the pipes in the kitchen had gone. Like the pump for the well water, the pumps for the filtration system for the swimming pool were damaged beyond repair, and had to be replaced.

We were not alone. With the canny exception of M. Caumont, who had put all his pumping installation in his cellar after a similar freeze-up thirty years earlier, all the local residents suffered almost as much as we did. The region has many holiday homes belonging to people from Paris and other northern towns, and from Bordeaux and Toulouse. Most of these owners had been warned but the thaw had come early in the week and they were unable to get away from work until the following weekend. When they did arrive, they found their holiday homes full of water, and with stained walls, and ceilings on the floor.

Outside the damage was catastrophic. Throughout the southwest, and even on the Mediterranean coast, mimosas died by the tens of thousands. Hardly one survived in Aquitaine. Mme Lambert lost her splendid lemon tree. A few palm trees sheltered by houses, or in the town centres, survived. One of ours, under the branches of a spreading chestnut tree, struggled on, the others, in common with the agaves, oleanders and the fig tree, gave up. Poplar trees more than twenty years old had their bark split by the cold, and the cypresses looked sorry for themselves. In fact, they were dying, but a tree can take a long time to die, and it was not until after the same performance was repeated all round the next winter that it became obvious that they were dead. Eventually we cut them down, making the garden in front of the house much sunnier.

But by the time the intense cold came again in the following winter, we had taken our precautions. I had spent long hours through the summer and autumn insulating every pipe I could find, putting boarded ceilings backed by thick fibreglass in the former pigsty which had become the filtration room for the swimming pool, and fitting an insulated door. I fixed a new insulated ceiling, plus wood-panelled walls, and a padded door to the pump room for the well water. As an extra precaution we emptied the swimming pool, drained the pumps and filters, drained everything in the pigeonnier and the fermette, and shut off the water supply to them. That winter we suffered no damage in the buildings, but outside the new mimosa which Marie-Anne had stubbornly planted, and the new Indian Lilacs (lagerstroemia) died. The bananas, which we had been astonished to see reappear in the spring as if nothing had happened, disappeared completely, only to reappear yet again the following year. I had cut down the apparently dead fig tree, which had been about fifteen feet high, but it, too, had started growth again from the bottom. It died down again, but the next year it once more sent up spindly growths and has since re-established itself, and is as fruitful as ever.

There was a third winter in succession much colder than normal, but by then almost everyone had taken precautions, and almost everyone we met told us that, of course, it was well known that a group of two or three very cold winters occurred in the region every thirty years or so. When we asked why, if they knew that, they had not been prepared for the first one, they just said that thirty years was a long time and people forget.

—

When we first arrived here, there was no such thing as a garden centre anywhere near. There were one or two nurseries where farmers could buy young fruit trees and vines, and which sold a few ornamental trees and bushes as a sideline. But after these hard winters, gardens and houses were so denuded of plants that everyone had to restock. At about the same time the French became garden conscious, and within the space of a couple of years a new industry was born. There are now five big garden centres within easy reach that sell everything that anyone might want to put in a garden, including large numbers of trouble-free, because artificial, plants and trees, as well as every conceivable form of garden furniture and garden tool. This is a significant change in the French way of life, and seems to be here for the long term.

In the short term it was the plumbers who benefited. While everyone else suffered, they rejoiced. When the thaw came, after the first freeze-up, they worked day and night, and were still putting things right in some holiday homes just before the summer season started. It was not long before the consequences started to show. If you saw a spanking new trade van, you could be pretty sure that the name on the side would have 'Plumber' underneath it.

We were rather impressed with the modesty of our own plumber who continued to turn up in his battered van, long after winter had finished. He had promised to repair the hand-pump for the famous mineral water. While investigating the damage I had realised that this pump, which someone had completely covered in anonymous grey paint, was in fact a splendid antique made almost entirely in copper, which took a beautiful polish once the paint had been thoroughly cleaned off, and with a fine cast-iron handle. The plumber had found a similar pump, disused in someone's back garden in the town, and proposed to take the necessary parts from it to reassemble ours. Rather sentimentally I bought it, and he, with a complete lack of sentiment or any sense of guilt, failed to make it work.

He was there trying again, unsuccessfully, early one morning, when the baker called. He is the only one in the area with a delivery round, and of course knows everyone's business in the houses he calls at, and since they report on their neighbours, and since his wife in the shop can serve four customers at once and gossip with all of them at the same time, there is very little the baker does not know about life in the village and nearby.

'What's he doing?' he asked, as he counted out my change.

I told him, adding, 'You'd think he could afford a new van with all the work he gets.'

The baker snorted. 'Hah. You would, if you didn't know he's bought his wife her own car, and he's having a new house built.' He firmly engaged gear and drove off in his own ancient little Citroën van.

Chapter Thirteen

New Wines for Old

Bacchus, the good-time god of wine, has been kind to this region. Apart from the vast vineyards around Bordeaux, there are large wine-producing areas around Bergerac to the north, around Cahors to the east, in the Armagnac area to the south-west, and around Toulouse. All these start within an easy hour's drive of our house, and only a little further off are the important vineyards of Corbières, and the Minervois, and in the foothills of the Pyrenees.

So you don't have to pay much for a decent bottle, only about half the going rate in London. Some of the Pecharmant wines, the best of the Bergerac area, are very pleasant, and even closer is Buzet (pronounced Byu-zay not Boozy) which produces a number of sound, vigorously marketed wines, and in the hills around Agen they make acceptable AOC wines. Closer still are half a dozen farmers within walking distance who, as M. Lambert did, produce and sell their own wines.

The Armagnac area produces ordinary wines, but some of the finest brandies in the world, and by going from farm to farm you can make your own discoveries among them. With all this vinous proximity, coupled with bargain prices, it is not surprising that some of the local inhabitants live in a permanent bibulous dream. Not least among them are some retired Brits who work hard to stop themselves getting sober.

France as a whole drinks more alcohol per head than any other country in the world, and about five million of the population, almost 10 per cent, drink far too much, and more than two million are already alcoholics. After heart disease and cancer, cirrhosis of the liver is the third commonest cause of death. The highest proportion of alcoholics is in a band stretching across northern France from Brittany to Belgium, and in the central eastern departments around Strasbourg and Colmar; but this does not mean that there are no heavy drinkers in the south.

When I first needed a mason, I knew nobody so I asked M. Lambert's advice. 'I'll send you someone,' he said.

A few days later one of those open-backed trucks drove up and stopped outside the barn. I went to investigate. The driver's door opened and a man fell out in front of me. He got to his feet with difficulty – he was very fat – and explained that he was a mason and M. Lambert had told him that I needed a job done. This speech, though perfectly understandable, was accompanied by an almost visible cloud of alcoholic fumes which, together with the fall, convinced me that he was about three-quarter seas over. As his face was that shining medieval, monastic purple which is not acquired overnight, I supposed that his alcoholic uncertainty was usual.

I did not reply at once. My mind, by association, had taken me back some years to the inaugural flight of a new American air service to the United States. The English public relations officer for the airline did us proud. Throughout the seven-hour flight there was a choice of whisky or champagne, interrupted only by an excellent lunch, accompanied by vintage red wine and brandy. Unwisely, he looked after himself at least as well as he looked after us. Eventually we arrived and as we taxied into position we could see a reception committee waiting on the tarmac, with a couple of drum majorettes in short skirts holding a banner with the airline's name. The cabin door opened.

'I'll lead the way,' said the PR man, moving unsteadily towards it.

Before he reached the bottom of the gangway he stumbled and fell, rolled the last few steps and landed in a heap at the feet of his new employers.

I felt a twinge of sympathy. He had tried a bit too hard, that was all. But one of my callous Fleet Street colleagues standing beside me said, with unkind humour, 'I've seen a lot of grovelling, but that's going too far.'

The PR man lost his job before we got into the terminus, and the woozy mason did not get one from me. I took the easy way out and said I had already found somebody. He drove off without hitting a gatepost. There was nothing on the back of his truck but two crates of M. Lambert's wine.

There is a big difference between the attitude of the average Frenchman to wine and that of the average inhabitant of the British Isles, and if it's an Englishman who fancies he knows a bit about wine, the two are poles apart. For most Englishmen, wine still has something special about it; to the Frenchman it's no more special than beer is to a Yorkshire miner. They know good from bad but essentially it's just what they drink and have always drunk, nothing to get excited about.

I remember when I was in Paris on business once, Marie-Anne's father invited me to dinner in his flat. He lived in one of those luxury apartment blocks where each flat has its own walk-in wine cellar in the basement. We had eaten some wonderful meals with him when his resident maid-cum-cook was on duty, but it was her night off, so he prepared the dinner himself. Nothing special, he opened a large tin of boeuf bourgignon (beef stewed with wine) and put it on a low gas, and excused himself while he went down to the cellar to fetch a bottle of wine.

He was a very cultivated man but totally without pretension. As a young man he had been an elephant hunter in Africa, and had lived a tough life. He told me once that he had often lasted the day on a handful of peanuts. Now that he was rich and could afford the best he bought it. He drank nothing but whisky and vintage champagne, a little red wine with meals, and tea, which we had to take him from Fortnum & Mason whenever we went to Paris. He was of Flemish stock and came from Rheims where his father had been in the champagne trade. There was always a crate of champagne at hand, supplied by cousins still in the business, and I knew I would be expected to split at least one bottle with him. He disliked ostentation, but as things turned out, he was wise to live well. A few years later his multi-million pound business, then the largest sawmill in tropical Africa, was taken from him at gunpoint by a central African government. He had provided a small town with model houses, two schools, two churches, a hospital, a covered market, a community centre and a sports stadium for his thousand African workers and their families. No compensation was ever paid and he died with little to show for his life's work.

But on that day, when times were still good, he came up from the cellar with champagne, of course, and a bottle of Château-Lafite 1961, one of the best vintages this century of one of the finest of all red wines. As he opened it, he broke the cork and the bottom third stayed in the neck of the bottle. He gave a Gallic shrug and pushed the remaining piece of cork into the bottle, saying, 'They have been together more than ten years. I don't suppose we'll taste the difference.' I certainly did not.

While it is not true to say that for the French, as far as wine is concerned, familiarity has bred contempt, it has certainly led to a healthy irreverence. Wine has been 'fiddled' for the best part of two thousand years. There is probably no other commodity in the history of man which has been subject to more persistent and varied frauds. In all the wine regions of France scandals are as regular as leap year.

The simplest fraud, which has occurred ever since bottle labels were introduced, is to buy a large quantity of decent, ordinary wine, bottle it and add an expensive looking label announcing that this is Château Whatsit, with a good vintage year date prominent. It is not that they try to pass off a table wine as a Mouton-Rothschild or some other great wine. The châteaux on the labels don't exist except in the commercial imagination of the swindlers. The wine is then sold direct to restaurants in Paris and the far corners of France and Europe. Some of the restaurant owners know what they have got but think their customers won't, and others are simply ignorant. There are, after all, more than four thousand châteaux making their own wine in the Bordeaux region alone. No man can live long enough to know them all, even in only their best years. This fraud, like most others, occurs as a rule in indifferent vintage years. Vintages have been good for several years and there has not been one of these scandals just lately, but it won't be long before there is another.

It has never done to have too much faith in labels. The wine in the bottle may be partly, or even largely, what the label says it is. On the other hand, particularly in hard times, there may be other things unmentioned on the label. As an example, in the 1860s the French vineyards, beginning in the west and spreading eastwards, were destroyed by the phylloxera bug. But it took twenty years or more to get from the Bordeaux region to Auvergne, and when the vineyards of Bordeaux and the Midi were already stricken, those in Auvergne were still healthy. So the wine-makers rapidly expanded their production to fill the gap, and if their wines lacked something in comparison with those of Bordeaux, they did not hesitate to provide it. If it was not fruity enough, they added raspberry or blackcurrant essence bought from the chemist; if it seemed to lack character, a little verdigris would give it a more pungent flavour; if the alcoholic content was too low, they would bring it up with sugar. Their wine was still not very good, but much better than none at all. Unkind people, no doubt wine producers from other regions, say that Auvergne wine is the reason why Orléans became the vinegar capital of France. This is because the wine used to be sent to Paris by river and canal in barges, but it was a long, slow journey and by the time it reached Orléans, it was often already vinegar. The Auvergnats say that the wine was so good that the bargees deliberately slowed up the voyage so that they could have a good drink from the barrels and top up with water.

On the whole French wine is not as good as it was. Wine is officially divided into four categories, which from the best downwards are AOC (Appellation d'Origine Contrôlée), VDQS (Vins Délimités de Qualité Supérieure), Vin de Pays and Vin de Table. These measures were taken in the hope of ensuring that the wines could be relied upon to meet the standards set for that class, and perhaps on the whole that result has been achieved. But, since the better the class, the higher the price, unscrupulous wine producers have been at least as ingenious as the Auvergnats were in 'improving' their wines. If in bad years their wine falls below the standard required, they find ways to bring it up to scratch. A scrupulous wine producer in France is harder to find than a bishop in a brothel and what the others get up to in poor vintage years is common knowledge throughout the industry.

One French writer has said that you would have to put a gendarme behind every barrel in France to stop 'frauds and fiddling', and even then some of them would not understand what was happening under their noses.

There are two other reasons for the decline in much French wine, more important than the abuse of the classifications. Both are linked to the success of the export side of the industry in the past twenty years or so. First, in all the regions which have produced successfully marketed wines, Champagne, Beaujolais and Médoc among them, the vineyards have been extended to build on that success. Often the only land available for this expansion was land that had not been put into vines in the first place simply because it was not right for them. The best wine comes from old vines on suitable land. When unsuitable land is planted with new vines, the combination results in indifferent wines.

The second big reason is that, where they have not changed the vineyards, some producers have changed their wines. France used to have a great variety of interesting and individual wines. It still has a great many different labels. The producers of their own individual wines envied the success of a few well-known wines which had caught on, and so they fiddled their own wines, trying to make them more like Beaujolais, or Sancerre, or Médoc, or whatever the case might be. The good, solid wines of Corbières try to be more refined, like those of Bordeaux, Côtes du Rhône tries to be like Beaujolais, and throughout southern and western France the white wine producers are striving to produce a 'poor man's "champagne"'. The result is that too many wines now resemble each other. Perhaps it is no coincidence that the consumption of wine in France is falling, while that of beer and whisky is increasing.

It is tacitly understood in the wine trade that more than half of all Burgundy has to be 'improved', or even largely substituted by wines of other regions before it can be sold at a price in line with the name on the label. A quarter of the Châteauneuf-du-Pape harvest goes direct, unbottled, to the Burgundy region. Wine brokers in the Bordeaux area regularly buy the lesser local wines and make them up into something better before bottling, as a rule using about 5 per cent of stronger wines from the Midi, or Algeria, or Rioja.

The commonest of all the frauds concerns the use of sugar. Other things being equal, and with serious drinkers even when they are not, wines with an alcohol content of 12.5 degrees sell better than those with 10. Extra sugar in the wine adds to the alcohol content. The law allows this to be done, but only in limited amounts and with certain wines. This is a regulation more honoured in the breach than the observance, if ever one was. Wine which, when fermented, may have had an alcohol content as low as 9 degrees regularly appears on the market at 12 or 12.5. Supermarkets in some wine areas sell, especially in poor years, up to one hundred times as much sugar in the month before the wine harvest as they do in other months, and some announce the arrival of their extra supplies on their public address system.

One cannot help being aware in this part of France of the irregular side of the wine industry. It is the middle and lower part of the range which is most affected. Only about 20 per cent of the producers of known wines, most of them at the top of the market, are reckoned to abide by the regulations. At the bottom end, they just make their wine. M. Lambert would never have dreamed of going to the expense of adding sugar to his wine. If in some years it was a bit low in alcohol, his regulars, like the mason, just drank more of it.

The capacity of some of the farm workers and artisans for wine is surprising. Every year the same three men come to prune our plum trees. The work is done in January or early February and takes three weeks, starting as soon as it is light and stopping when they can no longer see. Each of these men is a subsistence farmer, like M. Lambert, with cattle and cereals as well as some fruit trees, and they all make their own wine for their own consumption. They have been working together for years, but they still find something to talk about all day long, and in case they might run out of conversation they hang a radio in a tree, and include their opinions of the programmes.

I don't know how much they drink, and I have never seen one of them look remotely drunk, but their Gascon joviality goes full blast even at eight in the morning. I know that one day I got talking to them about wine and mentioned that I often drank half a bottle of red wine with my dinner. This really knocked them sideways.

'Half a bottle?' asked the foreman, incredulously. 'But that's very serious. You could ruin your health.'

'Oh, I don't think so,' I began, and then realised he was pulling my leg. He started to laugh, and the one who was actually in the tree guffawed and almost fell out, grabbing a branch to save himself.

'So how much do you have with your meal?'

'Oh, a litre and a half, perhaps two litres.'

He may still have been pulling my leg, but perhaps not. He's a big solid man, built like the trunk of an old oak, a real Gascon, and it's not so long since Gascon farmers took a barrel of wine with them into the fields to keep them going. Only a ten-litre barrel admittedly, with a neat iron handle on the side to make it easy to carry. 'Wine gives strength to weary men,' said Homer, and it's not the Gascon farm-worker who will dispute it. But clearly he doesn't think in terms of half bottles.

Another time, marvelling at the way they could keep going all day in all weathers, reaching continually above their heads, doing work that would cripple the average man in half an hour, I said to him, 'This job must give you pretty strong hands, squeezing those secateurs thousands of times a day.' He didn't say anything. He put his hand in his pocket and pulled out an apple – they eat apples and oranges at intervals all day. 'Have an apple, home grown,' he said, and held it out to me. Before I could say anything he closed his enormous hand and squashed it to pulp, the juice oozing out between his fingers. The others had stopped to watch this exchange, and now all three of them smiled with a touch of Gascon self-satisfaction. 'It's all the wine he drinks,' said the youngest of them.

Despite what has been said about fiddling wine, it should not be thought that blending wine is in itself a bad thing. Most everyday wines, like most whiskies, are blended, or what the trade calls 'assembled'.

The only Appellation Contrôlée wine which does not permit the entry of grapes grown in other regions into its cellars is champagne, which is produced under stricter controls than any other French wine. We have our own 'champagnes' in the south-west, sparkling wines made by a similar method but from a different blend of grapes, which will fire a cork at least as far as the real stuff. Regrettably, that's about all they have in common.

The complications of wine as a subject are infinite. As an example, Châteauneuf-du-Pape, though not a blended wine as such, is officially made from thirteen different grape varieties, and is itself often used to blend with below par Burgundies to tone them up a bit. In some wines the percentage of certain grape varieties is officially limited, but this is not the case with Châteauneuf-du-Pape.

A lot of nonsense is written by some modern wine writers. None of them would be likely to tell you that in a particular Châteauneuf-du-Pape, or any other wine, the characteristic flavour of one of the grape varieties used was more dominant than usual. On the other hand they will go to wild extremes in their subjective judgements of what the wine does taste of. I have even seen 'lush dollops of buttered blackberry fruit' quoted.

The guilty party may well have been Pierre-Marie Doutrelant, a French writer who nearly twenty years ago wrote a book called *Good Wines and the Others*, which says a great deal about the realities of wine production. In essence what he said about describing wine was that all that can ever be sensibly remarked about any particular wine can be said in everyday words. (There are about a hundred ordinary adjectives which have a specific meaning in relation to wine.) If your host offers you an ordinary red, you can, according to your level of politeness, describe it as hard, solid, robust, well-muscled, rich or powerful. If he offers you something feeble, you can call it banal, thin, light, discreet or, if you are very polite, delicate. The rest of what he said was meant to be light-hearted and a bit of fun. For example, he suggested a slightly different vocabulary for dining with an attractive woman. Then, the wine might be seductive, graceful, well rounded, sugges-tive, voluptuous, charming or any other suitable feminine phrase that comes to mind.

Or, and this is the point, if you want to bluff a pretentious wine snob, you need a poker face and, he says, your most serious expression while you examine the wine at length and eventually swill it around in your mouth, and then say that you find it has a slight taste of violets, or rosemary, or nutmeg, or cinnamon, or ripe quince, or unripe mangoes, or over-ripe figs, associated with a breath of hawthorn blossom. Take your choice. So long as you do not include onion or boot polish, he'll never suspect that you are having him on, and perhaps not even then. In England it seems wine writers have no sense of the ridiculous, or a sick sense of humour which they indulge at the expense of the ordinary wine drinker, presumed both ignorant and foolish.

Anthony Barton, the proprietor of the second-growth Château Léoville-Barton and the third growth Château Langoa-Barton, whose family have been prominent in the Bordeaux wine trade for 270 years and have lived at Château Langoa since 1821, says that when he started in the wine trade in the 1950s red wines were 'full and fruity' and white wines 'dry' or 'sweet', or, if you were brave and go-ahead, 'flinty'.

'I seem to have been left behind somewhere along the line . . . Now there's a whole new vocabulary which I find most confusing,' he says. In an article called 'A Wet Chihuahua', Mr Barton pokes gentle fun at the pretensions of some professional wine tasters. There is apparently a gentleman, kindly unnamed, who claims to recognise 218 different smells in wine and has listed them. 'Of all the smells that the expert is supposed to recognise in wine the one that baffles me most', says Anthony Barton, 'is Wet Dog . . . in the first place because it is apparently a perfectly permissible odour in any self-respecting wine . . . and the next point is "What breed of wet dog?" There is a world of difference between a wet chihuahua and a wet labrador. Unfortunately, when I mentioned this to the person responsible for this comprehensive, if incomprehensible, list of smells, he took me seriously. So we can expect an addition of fifteen or twenty new smells to the list, all doggy.'

I don't know what the pruners would make of it, if I told them professional wine tasters in Britain claimed that some wines have a bouquet of wet dogs. They would probably say something contemptuous about the well-known madness of the English, or crack a rib laughing, or by really falling out of the tree.

The heart of Gascony has its own wines, individual like much else about the region, and little known or almost unknown in Britain. Who in London knows Pacherenc de Vic Bilh, a pleasant white wine, or Madiran, a sound, full-bodied red wine which should never be drunk less than four years old and is better at fifteen? But the real Gascon drink is Armagnac, a brandy which at its best is nectar, and one of the most expensive drinks in the world. Armagnac was being made by Gascon farmers long before Cognac was developed. The soil, the balance of grape varieties used, the distillation process, the ageing, are all different between Armagnac and Cognac, but the greatest difference is in the producers. Cognac is produced by a few large companies and tends to be a standardised product at each of several levels from rough to superb, and is strongly marketed. By contrast, there are about 1400 Gascon farmers producing their own Armagnac in their own way. They don't like to join co-operatives, and they don't ask advice from each other. Some families have more than a hundred and fifty years of experience. Very few of them advertise, for their reputation has been made by word of mouth; over the years, they sell all they produce, when they are ready, and at anything from £10 to £300 a bottle.

If all this seems to be a diversion from life among the Gascons, I can only plead that neither wine nor Armagnac is ever considered a diversion in this region. Both are central to its life and everything to do with them is important and relevant. There have been many changes in production methods. The grapes used to be trodden in the vats – I remember seeing it done at Château Cantemerle, one of the last great châteaux to keep to this traditional method, about twenty years ago. Anthony Barton says his father remembered seeing the workers jigging up and down on the grapes to the music of a fiddler. On some estates, even among the great wines, the wooden vats have been replaced by stainless steel. But the biggest change is the mechanisation of the harvest on many properties, which is affecting the lives of hundreds of families for whom employment as grape pickers was part of the annual pattern of life. One grape-picking machine and its driver can replace forty pickers.

But, though there is modernisation everywhere, there remain some curious anomalies in the industry. The year after I helped with M. Lambert's grape harvest, we were in the throes of our first season of holiday visitors, so there was no time for grape picking. Instead, I asked him if he would like the grapes on the various vines which grew in odd corners around our house. There seemed to me to be quite a lot of them. He hesitated and then said yes, although my grapes were white and his wine was red. In the event I filled two large plastic dustbins with bunches of grapes and took them across to him. He allowed himself a smile at this insignificant quantity but said how nice it was of us.

One day the following spring, months later, I went to buy some new laid eggs from Mme Lambert, as I did each week. I met M. Lambert, stooped and hurrying as ever, in the farmyard. We shook hands and greeted each other with the usual formality. In this part of France, it is considered essential to shake hands with everyone you meet, not only as you meet them but also when you say goodbye. Then he said, 'I can give you back your grapes.' I had no idea what he was talking about and fancied for a moment that pressure of work was making him ga-ga. He disappeared into the house and came back almost at once carrying what looked like five bottles of champagne. Then he said what I can only translate as, 'We had to wait for the fizz-man to come round.'

A lot of the farmers in south-west France like sweet white wine – perhaps the sugar in it replaces the energy they use up every day – so they grow white grapes for this in their own vineyards. Some of them also like their wine bubbly. For all demands there is a supply, and a few men, there cannot be many of them, make their living as itinerant bubble merchants. They travel round the farms with a van fitted with gasifying equipment and put the bubbles into the wine the farmer has already made. M. Lambert had gone to the trouble of asking the 'fizz-man' to call to put bubbles in the wine he had made from my dustbins of grapes, and there it was, five champagne-shaped bottles complete with wired-up corks, gilt-paper cap, and an impressive blue and white label which says 'Vin Mousseux Gazéifié – Réserve du Vigneron – mise en bouteilles à la propriété – 1986' – all done on the spot by the bubble-man. Unfortunately, the wine itself was somewhat less gracious than M. Lambert's friendly gesture, but we found that it was quite popular as an iced aperitif laced with a good dash of peach brandy on a hot summer day.

In the past many farmers made their own eaux de vie and liqueurs from various fruits. When we first came here it was not unusual for people to call at the door asking if we had any eau de vie of plums for sale. At one time anyone could make their own spirits, then the right was restricted to certain families, in which it was passed down from father to son. Then, a few years ago, new regulations were introduced banning the private manufacture of all spirits, except commercially and under government licence. The farmers, of course, respect the law and if many of them seem able to produce a bottle of something special on occasions, it is always carefully dusty, and 'old family stock'.

There are still, in the Armagnac region, some itinerant distillers. The farmers who produce Armagnac sometimes have their own stills and distil the wine themselves, or they send it to the village distillery and collect the raw spirit from them, or they use the services of these men who travel from farm to farm with a traditional Armagnac still, as they have done for more than a hundred years. A Gascon writer, Joseph de Pesquidoux, has given a description of this important occasion:

As a little child then I haunted the 'chai' on distillation nights. I have known a renowned 'burner' operating on all our estates. One had to book a year in advance in order not to lose one's turn for the distillation. He arrived punctually; his feet in straw-lined wooden sabots, and dressed warmly with a woollen girdle to protect his kidneys from the night cold and a shawl or rug around his shoulders. Silently he saluted and at once took his place beside the alembic.

He was called Meste Jean (Master John) in order to indicate and in recognition of his incomparable fashion of 'burning' or distilling the wine. There was no need of any family name. Master John sufficed. I verily believe that all the countryside here knew his slow and slightly heavy step. Whilst he was at his distillation no one could get a word from him. All his being was engrossed in the noise of the wine which bubbled or boiled above the consuming wood. He had the air of listening with the whole of his being; his eyes half-closed, those eyes that the constantly watched and supervised flame had turned to a pale blue.

It sounds almost Dickensian, yet some of these men still practise their strange alchemy in the scattered farms of Armagnac.

The wine industry has been well able to afford its recent modernisation. It has not suffered in the recession of the past few years, only one year in the past ten has resulted in a poor vintage, and if home consumption has fallen slightly, exports have steadily increased. As an example, when we first came here nearly ten years ago our local wine co-operative at Buzet marketed three or four different red wines. Today there are at least a dozen, plus white and rosé. Extra vineyards have been bought or planted, and the overall production of Buzet is double what it was then. Ten years ago the wines of the Côtes de Gascogne were almost unknown outside the locality, now they are vigorously marketed, particularly in England. With the present drink/drive laws in Britain and France, the relatively low alcohol content of these light wines is a strong selling point. In another part of Gascony between Agen and Auch, the red wines of the Côtes de Brulhois, once little regarded, now have their own Appellation d'Origine Contrôlée. These are not isolated cases; the wine industry sails a pleasant sea of prosperity. But wine producers are farmers of a kind, and there is no such thing as a farmer with nothing to complain about. The weather is never right, prices could be better, the government should do something about foreign competition and imports, and so on. All the same the makers and brokers of wine are almost the only businessmen left who can reserve the word 'squeeze' for oranges.

Chapter Fourteen

WHERE'S YOUR GUN?

When the conversion of the pigeonnier had been completed, and when the swimming pool had been properly fitted out and put into operation, we decided rather timidly to see if we could get any holiday visitors, and if so, whether we enjoyed having them. We thought it would be easiest to try just for August. A single advertisement in the *Daily Telegraph* brought several inquiries, and we agreed terms with a family of three for the first fortnight of August.

On the morning of the Saturday when they were due to arrive I carefully raked the gravel of the terrace, and checked at least twice that there was enough bottled gas for the cooker, and Marie-Anne dusted the furniture and swept the floors and straightened the bedcovers, several times over. With her usual thoughtfulness and generosity Marie-Anne had decided that we should leave a 'welcome pack' in case they had had no time to do any shopping. So we left tea and coffee, milk, eggs, bread, butter, and a bottle of local wine. Eventually we retired to our own house to wait. The hours went by and nobody came. It grew dark, and we sat there waiting. Perhaps they were lost, perhaps there had been an accident, perhaps . . . what? In the end we went to bed, mystified. At about eleven o'clock on Sunday morning, the telephone rang. Our client was in Tours, about five hours' drive from us. He had been tired the night before, he said, and had decided to stop, but would be with us about four o'clock that afternoon. That was perfectly all right, we said.

Four o'clock came and went. No clients. But they arrived in the end at about seven, not three of them but five. 'Yes, well,' said

Dad. 'Nan wanted to come too, so we brought her, and this is my niece, Freda.'

'Oh, well,' we said, 'so long as you can make yourselves comfortable.'

'We'll be fine,' said Dad. 'Freda will sleep on the floor, won't you, Freed?'

'We brought the camp bed, remember?' said Mum.

In fact they turned out to be a pleasant, easy-going family, and we learned from them something that we have seen many times since – that everyone has their own idea of what makes a good holiday. Our splendid pool, so carefully prepared, was more or less ignored by all of them, except Freda. Mum and Nan sat in the shade knitting and drinking the occasional cold beer. Dad, who was manager of a car saleroom, and his eighteen-year-old son, Alec, who worked in a small factory making hand-built cars, seemed at a loose end until they saw me tinkering with a petrol-driven lawn-mower.

'Something wrong with it?' said Dad, hopefully.

'It should have two speeds, but the lever won't seem to stay in the "slow" position.'

'Got any tools, have you?'

I showed them the workshop. Since the power drill and the Black & Decker workbench, I had accumulated a good array of carpenter's tools, plus spanners, pliers, and all sorts.

'Hey, that's not bad. Didn't expect that, did you, Dad?' said Alec.

They put the lawn-mower right in a matter of moments. 'Anything else to fix?' asked Alec.

'Well, I have been meaning to have a go at these old bikes I brought from England, but I think they are too far gone. Nobody's ridden them for years.' One of them was a racing bike which had been a present for my son's sixteenth birthday about twelve years previously, and the other my daughter had ridden to school not quite so long ago.

That was their holiday. The sun sparkled unheeded on the pool and the river. The châteaux, the ancient villages, the caves, the historical monuments, waited in vain. They sat in the workshop, taking the bikes to pieces, cleaning, oiling, reassembling. When they had done that, they looked around for other things to mend. By the time they went home, there was nothing with moving parts on the property that they had not repaired. The only thing that defeated them was M. Rambaud's two-stroke lawn-mower.

The family that came for the second half of August were quite different, a professional couple with a son and daughter in their late teens. They loved the pool. Nigel, the seventeen-year-old son, who was an athletic, blond Adonis, with blue eyes and corn-coloured hair, seemed to spend hours ploughing up and down with a powerful crawl stroke.

I had told his mother that they could get farm-fresh eggs from Mme Lambert, and one day soon after they arrived, she sent Nigel on this errand. The result was surprising. Until then we had not been aware that there were any young girls in the neighbourhood, apart from Ginette, Mme Lambert's fifteen-year-old daughter who was charming but timid, and had not once dared to accept our invitations to use the pool. But that afternoon Mme Lambert telephoned us to ask whether Ginette could come for a swim, with a friend. From that day on, teenage French girls began to emerge from the bushes like day trippers from a bus. They were all, of course, studying English and, they said, hoping for English conversation. But for all that he was studying 'A' level French, they could hardly get a word out of Nigel. His minor public school was not one which, at that time, had relaxed enough to allow girls to attend, and he dealt with the situation with all the aplomb of a bashful young monk faced with a group of eager and near naked chorus girls.

Ginette and her friends kept trying but they were as awkward as he was, though they did not give up until he had gone back to England. When I asked Ginette later if she had learned any English, she just said politely, 'He was nice, but he didn't say much.'

We made several decisions that autumn. We felt that it had been a pleasure to have visitors, and decided to carry on. As we saw only French people for most of the year, we decided to concentrate on British holidaymakers.

The other important decision was that the fermette should be converted to a second holiday cottage. In fact it was another year before we started on it. This was mainly to recover our financial breath after the work on the pigeonnier and our own house, but we put the time to good use. Whenever we had some small job to do we called in a different tradesman, to see how well it was done, how reliable they were, what they charged and so on, with the idea of building a team to tackle the fermette conversion. Marie-Anne and I intended to do some of the less specialised work ourselves, nobody who had worked with the pigeonnier gang would be allowed anywhere near it, and one way and another we hoped to get it done much more cheaply.

As it was, the fermette consisted of two rooms, each about fifteen feet square, one a bedroom with a fireplace, the other a kitchen with a stone sink, a cold water tap, and a wood-fired stove for cooking and heating. On the far side of the kitchen from the bedroom was the 'chai', where in the past the farmers had made and stored their wine, and beyond that was a room which had contained the big oven for converting plums to prunes. Beyond the kitchen, the chai and the prune oven, at the other end of the building from the bedroom was the 'chauffeur's room', which contained a broken shower.

There was no guttering anywhere around the fermette, and the metre-thick outside walls had absorbed two hundred years of rising damp, visible on the inside. The roof tiles varied from dubious to rotten and the section from the chai to the corner of the prune room had been letting in the rain for years with the result that the wall, which appeared to have been made of biblical mud, straw and cow dung, roughly covered with plaster, was being washed away and had started to collapse. The loft above the ceilings was, as I mentioned, inhabited by firemen-frightening mice, and a tribe of football-loving and odoriferous martens. Apart from that there was nothing much wrong and to my starry eyes the place had possibilities.

I spent a lot of time that winter standing in this cold, damp disaster area mulling over the various problems, and drawing one plan after another. Some things had to be done whatever else was eventually decided on. First, the martens were tackled and, I thought, disposed of. Next, gutters were fixed all round the building. I had decided to have nothing more to do with the

plumber who had 'fixed' our antique pump beyond repair. The
new plumber, M. Rosetto, was a young family man with a
consistently cheerful manner, who always came when he said he
would, and did things properly and well. This work was done at
the end of spring so that the ground and the walls had the whole
of a long, hot summer to dry out.

The other key members of our new team included Pierre, the
genial, frog-eating mason. Despite his adopted French name of
Laporte, he was, like his cousin M. Zagillioni, of Italian descent.
Then there was the carpenter, M. Bonnet, totally Gascon, amiable
but unreliable, basically efficient but forgetful.

I have described our initiation into the occasional violent storms
which hit this part of France, and we made M. Bonnet's acquaintance following another such storm a couple of years later. It
happened like this.

When we first inspected the property with a view to buying, we
had been very taken with the beautiful Virginia creeper which
hung like a stage curtain from the cross-beams of the auvent, the
open canopy to the barn. At the time of our second visit, in
autumn, it was a glorious sight, flaming in red, yellow and gold,
and almost reaching the ground in places.

'C'est magnifique,' said M. Rambaud, quickly noting our
interest. 'There isn't another barn anywhere in the region with a
creeper like that.'

He was quite right. As events proved, the farmers had more
sense than M. Rambaud. While admiring the creeper, I had noticed
that the main cross-beam of the auvent had been reinforced with
an iron bar, and I mentioned it.

'Oh, that,' said M. Rambaud, easily. 'You know with a building
as old as this a little strengthening is prudent. It's nothing. Just
prudence. It is good for years.'

Well, it was. Two years. When you sign a purchase deed for an
old house in France, you had better look for, and you are sure to
find, a phrase which says that you accept the property as it is, with
all its 'vices cachés', its secret vices or, in more prosaic English,
hidden faults. Once you have signed that, if it falls down round
your ears, the vendor is safe from all legal action. M. Rambaud, of
course, had not failed to include this phrase, and Marie-Anne and

I had not failed to notice it. I was reasonably sure that there was a 'secret vice' in the barn, and I thought work would have to be done, eventually. It happened much sooner than we expected.

I suppose that, broadly speaking, there are two kinds of successful marriages. There are those where couples sail across a calm sea of agreement, never a cross word, and sometimes begin to look like each other, and even sound like each other, as they grow old. But there must be another class, even if Marie-Anne and I are the only couple in it. Our silver wedding is now in the past, and we have survived our years together in fire and storm and almost total disagreement. Love has veered to near hatred and back, we have called each other everything and terrible threats have been made. But they have never been carried out. So far, at least, there has always been an underlying attachment and harmony. When we were young we loved each other passionately; perhaps now we would admit only to deep affection and mutual respect. The fires may burn a bit lower, but can still flare up into violent argument.

Neither of us can remember what it was about, but on that Saturday afternoon we were livening things up with a refreshingly uncivilised shouting match in the kitchen. The storm outside we ignored until a sizzle of lightning and an immediate crash of thunder overhead was followed by another great crash of a different kind. It stopped us at once in mid-shout.

'Somebody's telling us to calm down. It sounds as if we have been struck by lightning,' I said.

We went outside together, tentatively. Most of the auvent was in a heap on the floor, tangled beams, tiles, vine, and part of the wall of the workshop which had been pulled down with it. One side of the roof of the auvent remained, looking as if it would follow the rest at any moment, and the two main supports were still standing though the great cross-beam had broken and fallen, despite the iron bar. Access to the barn itself was blocked and the whole mess was very unsightly. It would have to be rebuilt; the money would have to be found.

The man who had installed the filtration system to the pool, a retired colonel of engineers in the French army had, before he left, taken a look round the property, and had regarded us in silence for a moment, as if he was saying to himself, 'A likely pair, and no mistake.' Then he said, 'You'll never manage here. It will be too much for you. I think I know a young man who could help. I'll send him along.'

This was how we got to know Marcel, the industrial chemist turned forester. He turned out to be a godsend. There was no maintenance job he was not prepared to tackle, from fencing to mending the gutters, cutting the grass or felling trees, and everything was done well. To rebuild the auvent we needed timber, preferably oak, which even in France which overflows with forests is expensive. Sure enough, Marcel was able to provide and deliver exactly what was required at a third of the timber merchant's price.

It is typical of the south-west that I had no difficulty in getting a list of six men in the immediate neighbourhood who would be able to rebuild the barn exactly as it was done two hundred years earlier. Their ideas, however, of what it would cost varied wildly, though they were all expensive. One day I mentioned the problem to our friend the accountant, who lived on the other side of the Lamberts' farm.

'Try M. Bonnet,' he said, adding with a freedom I had never noticed among British accountants, 'he's a client of mine and he needs the money.'

I had taken three estimates from the six names I already had, and there was not much between them. M. Bonnet did not take long to decide that he could do the job, and his estimate was little more than half the most expensive one.

'It's a mess,' he said, 'but we'll sort it out.'

'Struck by lightning,' I said.

'No,' he said, 'struck by termites. This Virginia creeper looks marvellous, and it's all right on walls, but never on wood. It keeps it humid, and where wood is damp, you get termites. They tunnel away inside it. One day there's no strength left, and crash – simple as that.'

It was interesting to see how he and his son set about the job. First they propped the remaining roof up with telescopic iron tubes, as thick as drain pipes. Then they cleared the site. Next they lowered the two main supporting pillars to the ground, but still with the end of each resting on its flat stone base. Then they rebuilt the whole of the main supporting triangle on the ground in a horizontal position, with the great seven-metre cross-beam slatted into the holes at the top of the main pillars, and the side beams sloping up to the peak of the auvent, and linked to the cross-beam by smaller beams. The whole of this was then raised slowly from the ground to the vertical by a pulley system, until the base of the main pillars rested flat on the stones again. Next they shortened the telescopic iron props a few inches, until the weight was off them and was taken by the new wooden structure. Then they repaired the wall of the workshop, put in a new oak post beside it and placed another six-metre oak beam from the top of that post up to the nearest bottom corner of the triangle. From the centre of this beam, they put another great beam from back to front of the auvent, to carry the rafters on which the new part of the roof was reconstructed.

The whole operation took several days. M. Bonnet downed tools and said, 'There you are then, good for another two hundred years. Only get rid of that Virginia creeper.'

I did this by cutting through the main stems of the creeper, which were as thick as gate-posts, as near the ground as possible, with a chain-saw, and then covering the stump that was left with a generous dose of sulphate of ammonia crystals. There has been no sign of regrowth.

The broken and fallen beams were cut into logs and burned at once, with their hidden population of termites.

We had been impressed with M. Bonnet, whose work, though cheap, was sound. Though he was a real Gascon and therefore ready to cut corners if he thought you might not notice, he was also quite ready to do things as you wanted, if you insisted. So we had the mason, the carpenter and the plumber we needed for the conversion. Marie-Anne, by now an expert decorator, would do the painting, and I would make myself useful wherever I could.

The first thing to tackle was the dampness of the interior walls. This I did by gluing polystyrene panels, impervious to damp, to the walls, and then covering them from floor to ceiling in the natural pine strips called 'lambris'. All the wood was treated with a clear preservative against damp, fungus and insects. The result was entirely successful, not perhaps the decor for a Mayfair flat, but completely in keeping for a country cottage in this part of France.

It was obvious that the back of the chai and the prune oven, where the wall was being washed away and the roof collapsing, would have to be demolished, and then rebuilt by M. Laporte. To save money I decided that I would do the demolition myself with Marcel's help. I could not understand why, almost every time he saw me, the mason asked if I was quite sure I wanted to do that job myself. I wondered briefly if he was trying to make more work for himself, but though he had not been in business very long, he was quickly getting a good reputation, and already had as much as he could cope with. Marcel and I did knock down the wall. It took four working days to do it, and we practically crippled ourselves in the process. Only mule-like obstinacy saw us through. When it was done, I spent the best part of a week lying down, trying to recover my strength and waiting for my joints, all of them, to agree to bend again. When I saw M. Laporte, I told him how hard it had been. If I was looking for sympathy or compliments, I did not get them. He just smiled and shrugged.

'I told you,' he said, implying that masons' work should be left to masons. I only realised how over-ambitious I had been some time later, when we wanted to make a terrace for the fermette. The pile of stones, some more than a cubic foot in size, which we had so laboriously taken from the wall, was in the way. M. Laporte agreed to remove them. I watched him and M. Zagillioni pick them up as if they had been made of balsa wood and toss them one after the other into the back of his lorry.

I had been told that M. Laporte, now in his forties, had been a real Hercules in his youth and M. Zagillioni, who was a touch less modest than M. Laporte, said that he, too, had been a man to be reckoned with. As a youngster – he was now in his sixties – he had been a building worker and a marathon runner, and he told me that on the building sites nobody could work like him. 'I outworked them all,' he said, leaning for once on his spade and staring back into the distances of his youth, and adding, after a pause, 'easily.' They were a formidable pair.

For a time we were 'assisted' by George. Among the several

The barn with rebuilt canopy.

unusual 'outside' men who have helped around the place, he was rather special. He was a youngster not long out of school, and waiting for his papers for conscription into the French army. He had worked on Mme Lambert's farm and she recommended him to us as 'willing'. He was certainly that – he was so eager to please that he ran everywhere. If he needed a wheelbarrow, he ran for it. If I told him I had left an axe in the cabin by the river, he ran all the way there to fetch it, and ran all the way back. He seemed to be an Arab, but Mme Lambert, who was a 'pied noir' and had spent her youth in Algeria, said he was a Kabyle, and very proud of it. The Kabyles, she told me, are Muslims, but a branch of the Berber race. They are fierce, tough, mountain people, made of altogether sterner stuff than the usual North African, she said.

We learned two things quite quickly about George. One was that you had to be very careful what you said to him. You had to be precise. When Marie-Anne asked him to cut back a trumpet vine which was invading the guttering of the barn, he was so anxious not to disappoint he cut it to the ground. The other point was that he had a gift for breaking things. He would have had no trouble keeping a job testing things to destruction. Tools which I had used for ages broke or fell apart within five minutes in his hands. If there was an electric lead about anywhere on the ground, he'd find a way of cutting through it by accident.

I soon had to relegate him from helping around the fermette, in case he broke a window or dropped a brick in the bath.

'Let him cut the grass,' said Marie-Anne. 'He can't do any harm there.'

We were surprised. Having carefully explained the self-propelled, petrol-driven mower, I asked him to cut the lawns around the pool. He set off proudly. Some time later a friend, who had been sitting by the pool, found me and said, 'Don't like to interfere, but there seems to be something wrong with your lawn-mower. I think you'd better come before it blows up.' Completely unconcerned, George was striding rapidly across the grass with a lawn-mower emitting huge clouds of jet black smoke. I never found out what he had done to produce this effect. When I asked him, he just shrugged. He worked for almost nothing, but he was the most expensive help we have had. I was relieved when his papers came and he went off to the army. He hoped to train as a mechanic. If he did, and continued for his year in the forces as he had in the few weeks he was with us, I can only suppose that the French army now has numbers of military vehicles pouring out large clouds of black smoke, and others already on the scrap heap.

Once he had gone, the work on the fermette continued in more peaceful fashion. So far I had a bedroom and the basics of a kitchen. The old chai would convert into a roomy bathroom, and the larger area which had contained the prune oven would make a spacious bedroom, or perhaps, if the side walls were extended a few feet from where we had knocked them down, two bedrooms of average size. In the end we decided to extend the walls anyway, which would make the fermette slightly L-shaped and enclose its terrace nicely, but just to have a second bedroom cum sitting room, about twenty-seven feet by twelve.

M. Laporte extended the walls, and M. Bonnet put in a beamed ceiling. They were treated pine beams and, as I was not watching him, he put in twelve where eight would have been plenty, and carried some of them across into what was to become the bathroom, which really did not need beams at all. Gascons will be Gascons. Then he put the new roof on the extension, roofing being a carpenter's job in France. He also happened to have a huge window which practically filled the end wall of the new bed-sitting room, giving a view of the pool garden and the fields beyond. He let me have this at two-thirds of the catalogue price, because he had had it in stock for two years, after a dispute with the client for whom it had been ordered.

The kitchen was rather gloomy, having only a glass-panelled door on either side, and the one on the pool side opened into a dark porch. Marie-Anne pointed out that the logical place for the sink was where the old one was, and that any housewife washing dishes there would be doing it in near darkness. This was an exaggeration but I resolved the problem by cutting a skylight in the wooden ceiling and putting a glass panel in the space and immediately above that I took off some of the old roof tiles and replaced them with glass tiles, so that daylight shone down to the sink corner.

While working in the loft above the kitchen, I had heard a

strange cheeping sound from time to time. It sounded rather like fledglings in the nest, but not quite enough to convince me. I did not think it was rats, and I began to wonder whether the martens had returned to their old haunts. The top of the wall of the fermette facing the pool was a bit rough and ready with spaces in the eaves where the ends of the roof rafters rested. It was clear that any self-respecting animal that could climb a bit would get into the loft that way, so I asked M. Laporte to make good the eaves and fill in every gap.

'By the way,' I said, 'there might be something under the tiles just there. Don't know what. Could be birds nesting. Or it might be something else.'

'Dormice?' suggested M. Laporte.

There are plenty of these dozy creatures like fat, little grey squirrels in the region. They are of the edible kind, and were a delicacy in Roman times, when they were fattened up on walnuts and served at banquets. Though the local people have catholic tastes in food and there are plenty of walnut trees, roast dormouse is one dish I have never seen on a restaurant menu, nor have I found anyone who uses them in home cooking. Even M. Bonnet, a traditionalist in regional food who, like the gas man, hunts his own snails, has not tried them.

'Perhaps,' I said, in answer to M. Laporte. 'Or tree martens, possibly.'

'Hmm,' he said, obviously not much liking the idea of tackling martens at close quarters. 'If it's a female with young, could be nasty.' Long pause. 'Where's your gun?'

'Gun? I haven't got a gun.'

'What do you mean?' He stared at me in surprise. 'But everybody has a gun.'

This I knew to be more or less true. A permit for a shotgun is a mere formality and the great majority of the men in the countryside went shooting, and even those who didn't kept a gun in the house. Not only did they have guns, they used them right, left and centre. Farmers who shoot intruders without asking questions, brothers who shoot brothers in disputes about how to run the farm, husbands who shoot their wives' lovers, and lovers who shoot husbands, hunters who shoot other hunters in mistake for deer – such stories are the backbone of the liveliest page, headed 'Faits Divers', in the regional papers. Nothing much seems to come of the majority of these incidents.

There are still many peasants who do not trust banks and keep their money hidden in the house and if they shoot an intruder, particularly one known to the police, who is obviously there to steal it, no prosecution follows. In a recent case in northern Aquitaine, a market gardener fired on a group of men who were stealing his carrots, killing one man and seriously wounding his brother. The farmer was taken into custody. The following day two thousand local people demonstrated in his support and against the increasing lack of security in the area.

The consequences of an unpremeditated crime passionnel are also light or non-existent, so shotguns are part of the furniture in this corner of France.

'All right, then. We'll see,' said Pierre. 'Leave it to me.'

As it happened Marie-Anne and I went to Cahors on the day when he tackled this job, and were not back until late afternoon. The top of the wall was as good as new, without a space anywhere.

'Was there anything under the tiles?'

'A she-marten with three young. Don't worry, they're dead and buried.'

'What did you do? Fetch your own gun?'

'No, I didn't.'

Something in his tone, distaste, I think it was, stopped me from asking just what he had done.

'Well, the wall looks good. You've made a neat job of it. Nothing is going to get in there,' I said, and that was the end of our troubles with martens.

The fermette was nearing completion. Pierre had half-tiled the bathroom, and a new bath and loo had joined M. Rambaud's monumental basin and matching bidet, which I had rescued from the barn. Pierre had also spirited away the old stove in the kitchen and its extremely shoddy chimney, and had created a new chimney at eye level, by cementing short wooden beams into the wall and then fitting an oak cross-beam to them. All this was arranged so that an extraction hood for the new cooker could be concealed inside it.

All that remained was to find and install what they call in France an American kitchen – in other words, a fitted kitchen. These are still comparatively rare, having been discovered even more recently than bathrooms, and there are companies working their way through the telephone books offering to provide such kitchens to all and sundry at give-away prices. We are still getting such calls at monthly intervals.

There are several splendid joinery firms in France who make everything in wood that a house needs, except furniture. They have dozens of designs and sizes of doors, windows, garden gates, flooring, shelving, and so on, and about ten different kitchens in kit form, so that you can assemble exactly what you want in the space available. As the kitchen in the fermette would be used only five months in each year, I bought a cheap one, and planned to assemble it myself.

But the more I looked at the uneven floor, and the walls, which we had long ago discovered in these old houses are never quite at right angles either to each other or to the floor, the more convinced I became that I could never make a good job of it.

A rule which I have found works wonders is, when in doubt over a particular job, ask a workman you already trust whether he happens to know anyone who might tackle it. Make it clear that you want someone like him, someone who does a good job, someone who is, as they say round here, 'sérieux'. The chances are that he will have a cousin or a brother-in-law, or even a father, who might be interested. In my experience, the countryside of France is overrun with skilled tradesmen, who may or may not be retired, who are just waiting to tackle a 'black market' job, especially for ready cash.

I asked Pierre and sure enough he would mention it to a cousin, or more precisely, a cousin of his cousin, M. Zagillioni.

The man in question, M. Tolmezzo, was as far removed from the genial, operatic Italian of popular fancy as it was possible to be. He was thin, small, acid-looking, similar in mould to M. Bienvenue, the old plumber who had worked on the pigeonnier, but much less self-confident. He was also accent-deaf. If you do not speak standard French or preferably the very heavily accented Gascon form, people with this condition cease to hear you. The first unusual inflection throws them completely. I still have an English accent but as I am now used to being understood at once by nineteen people out of twenty, the twentieth, accent-deaf person confuses me and a somewhat crippled conversation can follow.

M. Tolmezzo asked me at least half a dozen times in different ways, just what I wanted him to do. He hesitated over everything. Yes, he had heard of that particular joinery company. No, there was nothing wrong with their products. 'En principe, ça devrait aller.' This is a favourite artisanal phrase which means that they cannot, as yet, see anything wrong with the proposal that has been made. It would have been better if I had let him do the measuring up, he said, it was so easy to make mistakes. It had not seemed to me so complicated. All that was required was an L-shaped fitment, with the sink and draining boards on the short side, and the cooker underneath the chimney in the centre of the long side, with storage cupboards on either side of it. The top had got to be level, ready for tiling.

From his attitude I was becoming convinced that M. Tolmezzo had never tackled such a job in his life, and was on the point of backing out. However, Pierre had confidently recommended him.

'Have you done a job of this kind before?' I asked, gently.

'Pardon. What's that?'

'I said have you done this sort of job before?'

'Oh, yes. It's my speciality.'

It took a little more patience to find out, but M. Tolmezzo was probably the most experienced man for this job in the south-west, having worked for a company who were very early in the fitted kitchen business, and where for the past few years up to his retirement he had done nothing but fit kitchens of all shapes and sizes, in houses old and new. His gloomy hesitation, I now understood, was based on experience and foreknowledge of all the horrible little difficulties the job was going to present. But he accepted.

He was one of those workmen who discuss problems with themselves, and I often found him chatting to himself. 'How am I going to get round this miserable bastard of a corner?' 'I should have started at the other end,' and so on. It was a pleasure to watch him work, and quite obvious that from the start he had the answer to all the rhetorical questions he asked himself. He put in beautifully neat strips and tiny wedges to make good the irregularities in the floor, and to make sure the work surface would be uniformly level. The final result could not have been better.

'I thought of doing that myself,' I said, after complimenting him.

After a week he was beginning to understand me. He looked at me and for once allowed himself an opinion.

'You did well to change your mind,' he said. 'That floor's as level as my potato patch. They just cemented it over without really levelling it.'

He was not there, though, to receive the ultimate accolade from Pierre as he tiled the work surface. 'He worked well, the cousin,' he said. 'He knows what he is doing, that one. He is serious.' Coming from Pierre, a man who, if he had the time, could build a cathedral on his own, it was a real compliment.

The fermette was a single-storey building with a low, uninsulated roof. The ceilings in the kitchen and the original bedroom were tongued and grooved pine, and though the reconstructed part now had plasterboard ceilings, and all the floors were about two feet below outside ground level – a primitive form of insulation – there was no doubt that it would become uncomfortably hot inside in the height of summer. There was nothing for it but to get up in the loft again and insulate it.

This was the last important inside job, and one which I foolishly undertook to do myself. First the whole of the floor had to be covered with bitumenised paper as a waterproofing. On top of this I fitted panels of compressed glass fibre – birds, mice, dormice, and so on, consider that the normal fibreglass has been laid especially for their benefit – about four inches thick, one against the other in a single layer all over the floor, using a short-handled broom, while lying flat, to push them into position under the eaves and in other inaccessible places.

Last thing of all was to make the floors acceptable. This was done by another member of the Italian clan, this time the brother-in-law of a cousin. M. Bricourt was not himself an Italian. He came from the Pas de Calais, where he had started as a coal miner at the age of fourteen. But in his twenties he had come on holiday to the south, and met his future wife. He came to live in the south permanently, where his mother-in-law had a restaurant in a small market town. Sadly, she became addicted to her own cooking and put on so much weight that she became more or less immobile, and could not stand long enough to make an omelette, let alone fifty lunches. So from being a miner M. Bricourt became a chef, but, unlike most Frenchmen, M. Bricourt has never had much interest in either food or alcohol. He eats when he is hungry and drinks water when he is thirsty. Nothing else. Cooking bored him, and when his mother-in-law died, they sold the restaurant, and M. Bricourt found a job as a carpet fitter and floor layer. He has been 'retired' for some years now, but is so busy that you need to book his services well in advance.

To round things off we made a gravel terrace twenty metres long and five metres wide along the whole front of the fermette. Marcel provided some oak and put up a post and rail fence to separate the terrace from the lawn beside the pool. My daughter promptly said that it made the fermette look like a stable, but if this has occurred to any visitors, they have held their peace.

This conversion of the fermette, using hand-picked labour and doing some work ourselves, took rather longer than that of the pigeonnier, but although it is the larger of the two cottages and was in a worse state of repair, the total cost was only a little more than half what the Pigeonnier Gang got away with. But at least we had learned from that experience.

Chapter Fifteen

RED DUST AND ACID

For many people one of the great pleasures in life is to relax either in or by the side of a pleasant, not too crowded swimming pool on a hot, sunny day. The sparkle of the sun on the water, the light swash and ripple from the filtration, like the murmur of a nearby stream, the stretch of blue in a green garden, combine to give a pleasure to the eye and ear that sets the mind at rest.

It took a good deal of persistent effort, and trial and error, before we managed to reach this state with our swimming pool. Even now, when I look at it on a beautiful day, I still sometimes see in my mind's eye that sinister pit overgrown by dark trees, full of decayed leaves and fallen branches, which M. Rambaud had allowed it to become.

M. Rambaud's eccentricities were legion but none was quite as extreme as this pool. It never fails to astonish people. It is not what you expect to find next to a country cottage. It is very large, larger than the majority of municipal pools in the department. In fact, you cannot see one end from the other, though this is because it is L-shaped, and whichever end you stand at, the other one is round the corner of the barn. The length of the water surface is in fact fifty-two metres, seventeen on the short arm, thirty-five on the long arm, though it is entered at either end by wide and shallow steps which reduce the swimming distance by about three metres at each end.

According to M. Rambaud the pool had been made by workmen who were 'compagnons', which was his way of suggesting that it could not have been better done. 'Compagnonnage' dates from the fifteenth century, when artisans in the same trade grouped together to strengthen themselves against their masters, to protect the secrets and develop the skills of their trade, and to find work for each other. A young apprentice could not become a full compagnon until he had made a three-year tour of France, where in each town he would be received by the local compagnons and would learn from master craftsmen. Compagnonnage was banned during the French Revolution, but revived soon afterwards. It still exists but its importance has been steadily reduced by industrialisation since the middle of the nineteenth century. The compagnons were respected throughout France for the quality of their work.

However, local people said that the pool was built, not by the compagnons, but by two itinerant Portuguese masons called Miguel and Antonio.

According to M. Rambaud the reason for the wide steps was that he had an aged uncle who was confined to a wheelchair but who liked to be pushed down them into the pool, and the reason for the unusual shape was that, having given instructions for the work to start, he accompanied the aged relative on a visit to a spa. When he returned he found that work had proceeded parallel with the river, though he had meant them to dig towards the river. The workmen dutifully turned the corner. Work was still in progress when he and the aged relative went off to another spa, without giving explicit instructions as to where to stop. When they returned, digging was still continuing, and had to go on for another three metres so that the steps could be made.

None of this sounds very like the 'compagnons' to me, but it's just believable of a couple of Portuguese masons, who probably understood very little French, and spoke less. A Portuguese family come every year from Portugal to help M. Caumont with the fruit harvest. They stay two months and have been coming for years, but none of them speaks anything but the most rudimentary French. So, on balance, my vote goes to Miguel and Antonio as perpetrators of the monster pool.

There are photographs to prove that at one time M. and Mme Rambaud did use the pool. The summers are hot and dry in the region, so when July comes the farmers start irrigating their fruit trees and cereal crops. M. Rambaud would wait until M. Lambert started irrigating the field beside the pool, and watch like a hawk as it proceeded, so that just before M. Lambert was ready to collect everything up and move on, he would call on him and ask if he minded filling the swimming pool. M. Lambert was much too soft-hearted to refuse, and within a day M. Rambaud had a pool full of river water. The Lot is a fairly clean river but it is no crystal mountain stream, and it was possible to see the bottom of the pool only at the shallow end.

My near neighbour, Jean-Claude, the accountant, who had then just moved into the farmhouse on the other side of Mme Lambert, remembers Mme Rambaud saying to him, 'Oh, you are welcome to use the pool whenever you like. We only charge one franc, but we think it advisable to treat the water, and so we also ask a standard contribution from all users to pay for the products needed. Of course, it is not a public pool, it's invitation only.' Not surprisingly, Jean-Claude, not yet being used to the Rambauds, did not know what to make of this, and thought it wiser not to take advantage of the offer.

Apparently the number of people willing to make a contribution to swim in adulterated river water was limited, and when we arrived, M. Rambaud had long since abandoned the pool.

The first thing we had to do was to get the setting right. The curtain of pines and cypresses, some of them with trunks more than two feet thick, had to be felled so that sunshine would reach the water.

Marcel, as a forester, made light of this task, providing enough logs to see us through several winters, and also cleaned out of the pool the years of leaves, twigs and fallen branches, and made bonfires of it all. Next the filtration system was installed with all the necessary underground piping. A former pigsty near the inside corner of the L-shape became the filter and pump room.

M. Filloneau turned up in his monstrous car with the gas bag on top and with a high pressure cleaning device in the boot, and blasted as much dirt as possible off the walls and the bottom. Once the water had drained away, this operation revealed that beneath the grime the pool was a mixture of greys, greens and yellows, with the odd touch of orange and brown. Here and there it looked as if Mme Rambaud, in a cubist mood, had started a mural on the sides, but most of it looked as if she had become bored with it, and just sloshed a bit of colour about. Whatever it might once have been, years of weather and neglect had obscured any recognisable design.

Marie-Anne thought that it might look a lot better once filled with clean water. I was in favour of painting it first, a conventional blue all over.

One day before we had resolved this question, we went to Bordeaux. There was nothing exceptional about the weather there, but when we got back in the late afternoon, the bottom of the pool was covered in a thick layer of bright red dust. So was Marcel's van, which was usually white.

Apparently, at about midday the sky had gone dark, as if there was an eclipse of the sun, a wind had whipped up and a dust storm had struck the area.

'Straight from the Sahara,' said Marcel.

It happens almost every year somewhere in southern France. Thousands of tons of sand, sucked up from the desert by certain climatic conditions, are blown across the Mediterranean and deposited on France. That year it was our turn.

We got out shovels and brooms and swept up as much as we could, but the whole surface still had a reddish tinge where the fine particles had stuck in the roughness of the concrete. We decided to have it professionally painted.

In retrospect I cannot think where we found the nerve to accept the estimate for this work. The combined surface area of the sides and the bottom, and the fact that the only paint suitable for pools was hideously expensive, plus the fact that it would take the best part of a week's work, meant that the estimate was well into four figures. There was no doubt about it, we could not afford it. But we were hopelessly committed. Metaphorically, we were halfway down one of those helter-skelters they used to have in fairgrounds, perhaps still have, where you sat on a mat and slid down from the top of a tall tower in a dizzy spiral and shot off at the bottom where someone waited to see that you landed safely. The only difference was that there was no one waiting at the bottom for us, except the bank manager, and he had an axe in his hand.

Marie-Anne, with the kind of feminine logic which can be very useful at times, said, 'Think of all the things we've bought in the past that we could not afford. There was no way we were going to be able to pay for our first car, and what about the loft conversion, and that month's holiday in Portugal?'

True. All paid for, and the agony long forgotten. Anyway, we could not go back. And a cottage with a swimming pool commands a higher rent. We would get the money back. Slowly.

So the trees were cut down, with the exception of two palm trees which gave an exotic touch, and the pool was painted a Mediterranean blue, and a man was found to clear the ground and plant lawns all round the pool. He was reluctant.

'I'll do it, of course,' he said, 'but it's all wrong.'

'What's wrong?'

'A swimming pool should always be at a higher level than the ground around it. It's more aesthetic.'

'How are you going to raise it?'

He looked at me. I looked at him. He went away and got on with the lawns.

He had a point. A swimming pool does have to be in the right place. A man bought a cottage not far from here with a long garden leading down to a small river, and put an eight-by-five-metre pool in the obvious place between the house and the river. It was summer and the ground was dry. In winter the river flooded and he had a floating swimming pool. It was some time before we discovered that M. Rambaud's pool, as we should have suspected, really was not in the right place.

People tend to take a swimming pool for granted. Having satisfied themselves that it is clean and not too crowded, they swim in it, and go away the next day or a couple of weeks later, and do not give it another thought. But when you live with a pool all the time, you never know what is going to happen next. I remember chatting to the manager of a famous hotel in Kenya, and complimenting him on the setting of the hotel pool.

'Oh, everybody likes it,' he said. 'Even the lions. We have to watch it carefully in the dry season. Mind you, they don't swim in it. They only come to drink it.'

As far as I know nothing comes to drink in our pool, but a fair number of creatures take an involuntary and fatal swim in it. Mice, rats, shrews, grasshoppers, ground beetles and bees are regular casualties, and on one occasion a hedgehog. The fields and orchards are full of life, and it's nature in the raw – everything preys on something else, and when a mouse is making a headlong dash for safety, he can be over the edge of the pool before he can say 'Minnie'. I go round with the net early every morning, and two or three times a week fish out some small animal.

To begin with, knowing that the winters would be mild, we left the water in the pool, thinking that if we put the filters on from time to time, the water would be kept sufficiently clean. People with more conveniently sized pools always do this, and also help to keep them clean by fitting a cover to keep out dirt and leaves. This is impractical for a private pool fifty metres long.

Our method was quite satisfactory until the big freeze-up in our second winter. When the thaw came, the filtration had broken down, and by the time it was fixed, the water was indescribably filthy. There was nothing for it but to empty the pool, hire the pressure cleaner, hose it all down and refill it. Or so we thought.

But having emptied and cleaned it, we found that our expensively painted pool was no longer blue, but pale grey.

By sheer chance the engineer who had installed the filtration system arrived that same day to deliver the various chemicals needed to keep the water free of bacteria and algae throughout the summer. At the time of the installation he had been working with a huge company of swimming pool specialists with branches all over France. But having been a colonel in the army and the mayor of a local village, he was more used to giving orders than taking them, and he quarrelled with everyone. The only answer was to start his own company, which he did.

Colonel Dallot was a small, thin, choleric man, efficient, and pleasant, so long as you let him do the talking. Usually he didn't talk, he expounded and you listened. He paid no attention to questions or interruptions, but merely carried on with his exposition. If, when he eventually stopped, you had a question, he would start again, more slowly, as if he were talking to a simple-minded child. He often prefaced his remarks with 'Écoutez-moi', and I got into the habit of referring to him in his absence as 'Old listen-to-me'. Once he had realised that, though English, I was not half-witted, and actually understood a lot of what he said, we managed to strike up a working relationship. Like all genuine eccentrics he had no idea that he was one himself; despite his temperament, and as he knew the installation better than anyone else, we always dealt with him. I got used to conversations full of exchanges like:

Me: 'The water seems a bit cloudy, but I have checked the pH and it's absolutely right.'

He (after a pause): 'That water's not quite clear. I've explained to you that the chlorine cannot do its work unless the pH is right. You had better check it,' and to make sure I had understood, 'Check the pH.'

Or,

Me: 'That pump sounds a bit odd to me, but it seems to be working all right.'

He (after checking a few valves): 'That pump sounds a bit strange. Nothing serious. Seems to be working all right.'

We had not known him long when he turned up as Marie-Anne and I were lamenting that our Mediterranean blue pool was now battleship grey.

'Écoutez-moi, Madame,' said the colonel. 'The water in this region is extremely hard. It contains a great deal of limestone. That's what that is, a deposit of limestone. The same as you have, no doubt, in your saucepans. Only you can scour a saucepan.'

'You mean there's nothing we can do?'

'Malheureusement, non.'

'When I think of what it cost, for just one summer. The cleaning, the labour, that special paint. We simply cannot afford to do it again. It's out of the question.'

'What special paint?' asked the colonel.

'Epoxy resin,' I said.

'Ah. You should have told me. Wait.'

He went to his car, fiddled about in the boot, and returned with a small plastic bucket, a black plastic bottle and a plastic sponge. 'I keep these for just such occasions,' he said mysteriously. 'Wait. Watch.'

One of the strange things that the Portuguese masons had managed to do was to tilt the pool very slightly from one side to the other so that when one end of the top step on the short side was just covered, the other end was bare. As it happens this has proved to be a useful indication that the water is at just the right level for the correct operation of the filtration.

The colonel filled his little bucket halfway and took it to the uncovered part of the top step which, as it was sometimes covered, was also grey with limestone deposit. He carefully unstoppered the black plastic bottle and poured some of its contents into the water in the bucket.

'Hydrochloric acid,' he said, impressively, like an alchemist about to turn a house brick into a gold bar. 'Now, watch.'

He took his sponge and dipped one end of it into the bucket, and then pressed it on to the bare step. The step bubbled and fizzed where he had touched it. He splashed a little water from the pool on the place, and lo and behold, it was blue again.

He did not say 'Abracadabra.' He said, 'Et voilà,' and then poured the contents of the bucket on the step. It fizzed some more, and he washed it with more water, and a patch as big as a saucer became blue.

'That can't be very good for the paint,' said Marie-Anne.

'Madame. Plastic bucket, unharmed. Plastic bottle, unharmed. And on your pool plastic paint, untouched. Hydrochloric acid eats away most things, including metal and stone, especially limestone, but it has no effect on most plastics, and epoxy resin paint is plastic based. All you have to do is to wash your pool down with a mixture of hydrochloric acid, one part of acid to two parts of water, and then rinse it with clean water, and your pool will be blue again.' He spoke as if he were telling us how to wash a cup and saucer.

'Is that all?' I asked. 'Won't it take rather a lot of acid?'

'It's a big pool,' he said. 'Sixty litres, perhaps more. Nasty job but a lot cheaper than painting.'

So began the acid saga. Marie-Anne and I decided to do the job between us. But first I had to buy the acid. I received some very strange glances and was discreetly interrogated when I asked for three thirty-litre drums of hydrochloric acid, which was, apparently, a convenient amount for putting in a bath to dissolve the body of an unwanted rich relative. I managed to persuade the salesman that I had no such ghoulish intentions, but needed it for the entirely innocent purpose of cleaning the limestone from my swimming pool.

Having provided ourselves with acid-resistant plastic wellies, plastic gloves and capes, Marie-Anne and I set to work. It was a terrible job. First of all I made the mixture in a plastic bucket, then poured it into a plastic watering can and then, beginning at the shallow end, so that it would run down the slope, sprayed the mixture across the width of the pool.

Marie-Anne followed with a plastic squeegee, wiping and mopping, as if she were washing the kitchen floor, and when I had emptied the watering can, I picked up another squeegee and helped her. Two filled watering cans would do the best part of a metre. Then more mixture. Repeat exercise fifty times, stopping every five metres or so to follow the same procedure on the side walls.

It took the best part of a week to finish and then pump out the accumulated dirty water, hose down with clean water, and pump out again, ready for filling. Most of the time we were 'enjoying' an April heat wave, which down here means temperatures in the high seventies, and the bottom of an empty swimming pool in a heat wave is a minor variation of hell. In the end we used 150 litres of hydrochloric acid.

Marie-Anne swore she would never go near the pool again, and certainly never to do that job. But I knew that it would have to be done again. The only water we had to fill the pool came from the well and the spring, so by the end of the summer there was bound to be another coat of limestone over the blue. I spent a lot of spare time during the winter telling myself that there must be a better way to do that job, and trying to find the answer. It came to me one day while I was spraying the fruit trees against disease. The seven-litre container I was using was a nice bright yellow plastic. Why not put the mixture in that and spray the pool instead of sluicing it from the watering can?

When the time came, I tried this method and it worked beautifully, reducing by two-thirds the amount of acid needed, and by half the amount of time necessary. By this time familiarity with the acid had bred a certain amount of contempt, and apart from the plastic wellies we had given up wearing protective clothing in favour of comfort. It was not until some time on the second day, when my face and forearms had been prickling for a quarter of an hour, that I realised that somehow I was spraying myself with acid. The reason was that the tube which led from the trigger mechanism to the actual jet was made of light metal, though everything else was plastic, and the acid had eaten tiny holes into the tube, from which fine jets of acid were spraying in all directions.

I tried every ironmonger and garden supply shop for miles around searching for a stiff plastic tube that would fit. No such thing. In desperation I racked my brains, looking in dark corners of the barn and workshop, hoping that what I wanted would suddenly materialise before my eyes. It did. Several times, but at first I didn't see it, because it was metal. As a result of the freeze-up, burst pipes, and so on, and because I am one of those people who keep all kinds of things in the belief that they may be useful one day, I had put aside some copper piping which the plumber had taken out and replaced. Staring hopelessly at this, I suddenly realised that it looked to be about the right size. By some miracle it proved to be, not about the right size, but exactly the right size. I cut a piece, longer than the original tube, so that I would be further from the acid, and fitted it. It worked and has continued to work perfectly. The acid, for reasons which seemed miraculous to me but no doubt chemists can explain, has had no apparent effect on the copper.

So now we knew how to keep the pool blue. But Marie-Anne, who still hated this job, said one day, 'Why don't we try to find someone to paint over it, instead of spraying it?' We had realised by this time that there was often a great difference between one price and another for the same job. It was not long after we had finished the fermette, and M. Bricourt, who had painted the outside wall, as well as laying the floors, seemed a possibility.

I asked him. He had seen the pool, but he accepted without hesitation.

'It's a big job,' I said, wanting to be sure that he knew what he was tackling.

'Any big job is just a lot of little jobs one after the other,' he said, a useful and understandable philosophy for a man who started life getting out tons of coal a shovelful at a time.

As a compromise, we decided to give the whole pool a less thorough cleaning and to have only the bottom repainted. Since M. Bricourt completed the painting in less than two days, and charged rather less than a tenth of what our first professional had charged, we are continuing with this policy, painting the sides one year and the bottom the next.

So there was this lovely blue pool, filled with crystal clear water, surrounded by green lawns, and splashes of purple and pink from four large tubs of petunias, and happy parents on their sunloungers watching happy children playing in the water. At last, we thought, we had won.

Not quite. After a long hot spell there was another Gargantuan storm early one morning. The rain fell in sheets, like Niagara in the wet season. No problems in the house. No problems in our garden, except for a few plants temporarily beaten down, and the goldfish pond flooded on all sides. But when I went to look at the swimming pool, the water was totally, from one end to the other, a deep, rich chocolate brown.

This was when we realised that the swimming pool was not in the ideal place. The orchard was at a slightly higher level than the pool garden which was reached down a gentle two-foot slope. It had been enough. When heavy rain falls on our clay soil it is absorbed very slowly, and in a violent storm it just runs off the surface. In this case a river of mud had poured from the orchard, down the slope and straight into the pool. I have since put this right, I hope. After a longer than usual drought, the lawn burned away to nothing and had to be replanted in the autumn. When this was done, the soil was cunningly sloped up from the middle of the lawn to the edge of the gravel surround which borders the pool, so that if a similar thing happened again it would be the lawn that was flooded, rather than the pool. But at the time of the disaster there were more urgent problems. There were families on holiday in both cottages and the pool was unusable. Only eels would have enjoyed swimming in it.

Marie-Anne rang up Colonel Dallot, since he understands her French rather better than mine, and explained what had happened. She reported his reaction as 'Do not panic, Madame. There is an answer to every problem,' and he proceeded to tell her what it was.

Following his instructions we filled a plastic dustbin with water and dissolved about two kilos of sulphate of aluminium powder in it. The solution was poured into a large watering can and sprayed over the surface of the pool, and this had to be done five times to make sure that as much of the surface as possible could be reached.

Sulphate of aluminium is a coagulant, Colonel Dallot had explained, and would sink to the bottom carrying the impurities with it. When all had settled, all I had to do was to fill the pool to the edge and then vacuum clean it, sending the dirty water direct to the drains, instead of back into the filter. His exposition made it clear that, if I did not fill the pool to the top, the water would fall below the level at which either filtration or vacuum cleaning were possible.

Sure enough the pool still looked horrible the next morning, but mostly because there was two inches of mud on the bottom. The water near the surface was a lot cleaner, but after vacuum cleaning it was still far from right. 'You may have to do it twice,' had said Colonel Dallot. In fact I had to repeat the whole operation three times, over three days, and then it took another three days of filtration, and repeatedly backwashing the filters, before the water was back to normal.

The pool has caused us a lot of worry, but this has been far outweighed by the pleasure it has brought to people. It's true that some visitors never swim, but the majority have great fun, each using it in their own way. We had one hard-pressed television executive who felt that, in order to be that bit sharper than his rivals, it was important to be that bit fitter. Every morning he swam a hundred lengths of crawl non-stop, then got out, towelled off, put on a track suit and, whatever the temperature, ran to the village and back, a distance of about four miles. A lady solicitor felt that fifty lengths followed by a two-mile run was enough to keep in good form. One vegetarian guest demonstrated his stamina by doing a hundred lengths daily and also rowing long distances on the river. This couple were crusading vegetarians who repeatedly told us and other guests that they 'abstained from dead flesh'. Another guest got slightly fed up with this and one day recommended to them a restaurant where she and her husband had dined the evening before. With a straight face she said, 'We had some really superb dead flesh as the main course, rib of beef, beautifully cooked, just a little bloody in the middle.'

We have been impressed by the athletic performers in the pool, and by the somewhat less athletic. One highly stressed business executive rarely went in it, preferring to lie beside it with a book, which soon sent him to sleep. On waking, having recovered some strength, he would get up to launch an electronically controlled model of the *Queen Elizabeth*. He then sat down again and steered it round the pool by remote control, until he was exhausted, and then lay down again. He went home much restored. What we have enjoyed most is that two small children and one nervous middle-aged gentleman have learned to swim in it. And all the worry and exhaustion it has caused us has been amply repaid by the many pleasant evenings of drinks and barbecues on the grassy lawns beside it, and the luxury of swimming during heat waves in the delicious coolness of what is, after all, practically mineral water.

Chapter Sixteen

A-Hunting We Will Go

Or perhaps, fishing. At first sight there is nothing very blood-thirsty about the appearance of men like M. Laporte, or M. Zagillioni, or M. Roucas, our genial and easy-going local mayor, whose basic political principle of 'Don't interfere with people' has got him re-elected repeatedly over the past twenty years. But they, in common with many of the local male population, are ardent hunters.

For hunting read, in the English sense, shooting. 'La chasse', in southern France at least, invariably means shooting, and there isn't a pack of foxhounds within a hundred miles. There are a few foxes, but they also get shot.

'La chasse' is a male preserve. Women are not actually banned from shooting, but none of the local clubs has a woman member. Their participation is confined to preparing for the pot whatever the hunter brings home which, in general, does not seem to be much. The hunters are often in groups of two or three, each of whom may have his own two or three dogs with him. The dogs whine and bark a great deal, and the men shout to each other, and blow a special whistle which reproduces a sound like a toy steam engine, though it is supposed to be a bird call. They seem to do all they can to frighten every animal within the square kilometre into taking cover. All the same, they do a good deal of shooting, with the result that they manage to hit some of their own number every season, and recently, even a cow which had strayed into some bushes at the edge of a field and was mistaken for a deer.

The hunting season normally runs from the second Sunday in September to mid-February, but for certain birds and animals it is much shorter, and in some areas hunting is permitted only on certain days. Near us it is Thursdays, Sundays and public holidays. An individual hunter is supposed to ask permission of the farmers or landowners where he wants to shoot, but rarely does so. In practice almost all hunters belong to clubs and permission is sought at club level. Club members pay a subscription, an important part of which goes to buy game for release in the shooting areas. There are several pheasantries in the region, in each of which hundreds of birds are bred annually. They are released a day or two before the season opens. Finding themselves outside the security of their cages, the birds tend to wander about in a daze, wondering what to do next, until a dog or a hunter disturbs them, when they whirr off in a panic and the guns blaze away. Within a couple of weeks they are all dead. In some places so-called 'wild' boar are also bred and released for the benefit of organised hunts.

The general shortage of game is such that some big landowners, who breed their own game, offer a day's shooting to the hunting clubs. Lunch is included and each hunter is guaranteed a 'bag' of three 'heads' to take home, whether he actually shoots anything or not. The price for the day's outing varies, but is never cheap, and is out of reach for most ordinary hunters. When I mentioned this aspect of hunting to M. Zagillioni, a faraway look came to his eyes, as if I'd suggested a cruise to the Caribbean.

Attempts are being made to increase the amount of game in the area by importing couples, particularly wild goats or hares, from other countries and leaving them undisturbed for a few seasons in reserved areas. Eventually, hunting is permitted but only in controlled shoots.

For everyday hunting the first and last days of the season are the busiest. In our first autumn here I remember being woken up early one Sunday morning by what I thought at first was a firework display, but which, as the pellets began to patter down on the roof like hail, I realised was the opening of the hunting season.

We soon became used to the general philosophy of the local hunters which seems to be 'If it moves, shoot it,' or at least 'Shoot at it.' On Thursdays and Sundays the shots rattle on all day, and although game is plentiful, it is impossible to believe that anything but a fraction of them actually hit anything. Since I banned hunting in my fields, I frequently see hunters crossing them and I sometimes go and chat with them and remind them gently of the situation. I have not yet met one who has killed anything, and despite the fact that there are rabbits in all the fields and orchards in the locality, the only time I have ever seen a dog with a rabbit in its mouth was outside the hunting season, when a neighbour's dog emerged from a field of young maize just in front of me. He was so startled that he dropped the rabbit and bolted.

At the end of a frustrating day the hunters are inclined to shoot at anything. As the light fails the guns continue to pop. Like those drivers who can see through fog, there are apparently some hunters who can see in the dark. I have been outside in the late twilight when I could barely see from one plum tree to another, let alone whether there was a pheasant snoozing among the branches, but the guns continue. Strangely enough, at that time any shot is immediately answered by another in a different area, as if to say, 'It's not only you who can see in the dark.'

Mme Lambert, who, in the old tradition, keeps about a hundred pigeons in a pigeon-loft attached to her barn, says that every year the hunters shoot some of them, and that occasionally they get a duck, and once a goose. She and M. Caumont continue to allow shooting on their land, though no one in these families ever hunts.

But no one in the countryside of France ever makes fun of hunting. It is too important politically. Sheer numbers make the hunting vote crucial in many localities. When hunting is attacked, it is on ecological grounds, not for its farcical aspect.

The two chief bones of contention are bears and wild pigeons. There are only about a dozen bears left in the Pyrenees and both the French government and the EEC are in favour of conservation, and of reintroducing bears. This has been done successfully in the Aosta valley in the Italian Alps in an area where there are sheep farmers. But in the Pyrenees hunters are opposed to the reintroduction of bears, because a large area would have to be set aside for them, and all hunting within it would be banned. Farmers are opposed to bears because they do kill sheep, although many more are killed by stray dogs.

There is also fierce argument between hunters and ecologists over wild pigeons. At certain times every year flights of thousands of pigeons cross the Pyrenees and are caught with nets and lures, and by shooting. Considerable numbers are killed. The EEC has issued directives seeking to control the numbers taken. The hunters say this 'sport' is traditional. The ecologists point out that not all that is traditional is good. The persecution of witches, sometimes to death, was traditional throughout the Middle Ages, but was abandoned. It is not suggested that shooting should be stopped, only that it should be kept within limits. At present it is more prevalent than it used to be, because four-wheel-drive vehicles enable the hunters to get higher and higher in the mountains and within shooting range of the flights of pigeons. Landowners are now renting 'palombiers' (hides from which to shoot) for thousands of pounds a year, rather in the way that stretches of Scottish salmon rivers are rented out. At this level it is now a sport only for the richest societies and individuals. The local hunters in the Pyrenees usually cannot afford it, and also dislike being told how many birds they can shoot by officials who live a thousand kilometres away in Brussels.

The ecologists also like to point out that cars and deep freezes have altered hunting. In the past a man would shoot a rabbit for the pot, and eat it within a day or two. Now he takes his car to within a few hundred metres of where he means to shoot and, if he can, he will fill the car boot with what he bags, knowing that he can put it all in the deep freeze. The same applies to fishermen. The animals and the fish may remain in the deep freeze for months. If some of them were still in the woods and the rivers, they would be proliferating, and there would be more for another occasion. While the arguments go on, the hunters continue to bang away.

We put up with the Sunday cannonade for some time, despite the fact that, though hunters are not supposed to come within a hundred metres of a habitation, we used to find them hiding behind the garden fence and shooting over it. The hail of pellets did not bother us too much. The final straw was when a thwarted hunter, unable to hit anything moving, shot the glass out of a floodlight set in a pine tree to enable us to light up the pool on warm summer nights.

Anyway, the following season I put up 'Propriété Privée –

Chasse Interdite' notices. M. Caumont warned me that it was dangerous, and that revenge might be taken in the form of damaged crops or plants. Nothing has happened except that a couple of the notices were shot down and thrown in the under-growth. I retrieved them and put them back.

The problem now is that we have too many rabbits. I may have to do what M. Caumont did. He invited the local hunting club to have an open weekend on his land. About twenty hunters turned up with an army of dogs and ferrets, and after two days had shot eight rabbits.

Fishing, by contrast, is not a noisy occupation. Both parties, fish and fisherman, maintain a dignified silence throughout. Many anglers are still for long periods, as well as silent. Once when I took my son out in the boat on two successive days, and we passed the same angler, in the same purple pullover, installed on the same seat in the same place, my son said, 'I don't think he has moved since yesterday.'

The Lot is a superb fishing river, and a remarkable river in many other ways. Except that it does not flow into the sea it is a model of all that a river can be. Starting off as a babbling trout stream in the foothills of the Cévennes mountains, in the southern Massif Central, it cuts its way through limestone plateaux in spectacular gorges, and then sweeps in great loops, like the one which encloses Cahors, past ancient towns, and is crossed by old and picturesque bridges, in the shade of which, in the upper reaches, fat trout idle. Below Cahors, the valley opens out slightly and limestone cliffs are gradually replaced by the wooded slopes of gentle hills, crowned here and there by a castle or an aged stone village. Then the valley becomes wide and sunlit, and on the gentler slopes are the vineyards which produce the well-known Cahors wines.

About twenty years ago barrages were built on the Lot, changing the lower reaches into a river which, in summer, is deep and slow-flowing, at times as still as a lake. Both east and west of us the river flows between steep, tree-covered banks about thirty feet high, and with a belt of trees along the top. Behind this narrow belt there are farm fields or orchards on both sides of the river. In a stretch of about four kilometres near us only a couple of farm buildings and an old manor house can be seen from the

river. The trees, the tangled undergrowth on the banks, and dead trees which have fallen here and there into the water, make a perfect habitat for birds and river animals of many kinds. Wild duck, moorhens, kingfishers, herons and buzzards are common, and the banks are the home of numerous small animals from the coypu down to the water rat. It would have been a perfect setting for the meeting of mole and water rat in *The Wind in the Willows*.

The fifty-kilometre stretch of the river before it joins the Garonne at Aiguillon is packed with fish in variety and numbers. Bream, roach, zander (pike perch), black bass, carp, pike, perch, eels and the ubiquitous catfish are the commonest. There are also plenty of freshwater crayfish.

Some of our visitors catch a lot of fish. One man on a fortnight's holiday fished for a couple of hours most evenings, and caught altogether more than a hundred fish. Unlike the French anglers, he put every one back. Others do less well. An expert angler who has travelled all over England fishing for carp and has won prizes, failed to catch anything at all in his first week, and became more and more sulky, especially when I told him that only the day before he arrived a twenty-eight-pound carp had been caught from Mme Lambert's river bank. At the beginning of his second week I saw him coming back from the river with a smile on his face. He had caught a sizeable bream, and from then on things improved, but he never did catch a carp.

One man fished for a couple of hours from the platform which Marcel and I had made using the old gas-piping gate as reinforcement for the concrete, while his wife sat in the shade at the back of the boat, which is moored to a tree whose tangled roots reach out into the water. He didn't catch anything, but his wife, having put down the book she was reading, and being sharp-eyed and quick, caught a dozen crayfish with her bare hands as they moved among the tree roots. She took them back to the cottage and that night's supper included crayfish salad.

Along both banks of the river in these lower reaches, there are fishing platforms every hundred metres or so. They are mostly rickety affairs, some on old oil drums lashed together, some wooden, some collapsing into the river. Every year as the fishing season starts, the sound of saws and hammers can be heard along the river, as each angler builds his own platform or patches up an old one.

When all is ready they sit, often in an old car seat fixed to the platform, and wait in what seems, to the casual observer, to be a state of optimistic somnolence. There are important differences between fishing in France and fishing in Britain. To begin with, in France the optimism is much more often justified. I remember having to write an article on angling in Britain in the late 1970s. According to my researches it was at that time Britain's most popular sport, with about four million anglers. Unfortunately there were not nearly so many fish, as pollution had killed them all off in some rivers, and they were dying rapidly in others. Every year more and more anglers were fishing for fewer and fewer fish. Fishing competitions could sometimes be won with a few ounces of fish, and at the end of the day some competitors had caught nothing but rusty buckets, old corsets and the odd bicycle wheel. There was considerable interest when an angler in Sussex caught five gold watches, a locket and a gold chain. If a school of gold watches, why not a shoal of diamond rings, or a spiny tiara lurking like a lobster in some dark cranny under Brighton pier? But no, after that one glint of gold from the murky depths, British anglers were soon back to catching nothing or little, and being obliged to put back what they did catch. I believe that conditions have improved since then, and that rivers are cleaner than they were.

The situation is utterly different in France where there are still thousands of miles of unpolluted rivers and countless lakes, all swarming with fish. Unlike anglers in Britain, the French angler throws nothing back, unless it is beyond all doubt inedible, or frankly under the minimum size allowed.

M. Noir, who helped us in the garden one summer, was an enthusiastic angler. He had very little enthusiasm for anything else. He had been in the army for many years as a private, and was a fine example of the fact that people in the same occupation for many years, whatever their race or country, end up more like each other than like many of their fellow countrymen. He was a typical regular soldier and had brought grumbling to a fine art. Nothing was ever right for him. When I showed him the admittedly untidy workshop where the garden tools are kept, he said, 'This workshop is a disgrace.' If I handed him a tool, he would look at it sourly and say, 'It's blunt,' or if I asked him to cut the lawn, he would start the mower and then say, 'Listen to that. It's time this motor was tuned.' He drank like an Irish writer and smoked like an old bonfire, always with the last charred half-inch of a hand-rolled fag in the corner of his mouth. He suffered with his health and the biggest mistake was to ask him how he was. He could take twenty minutes to tell you, and it was never good. He'd torn a muscle in his leg and could barely walk, or he'd had a feverish cold and was not really recovered, he'd got lumbago and couldn't bend, or his blood pressure had surged and the doctor had advised him to take things easily. He also seemed to be accident prone. He had not been with us long when he slipped a disc and was out of action for several weeks, and soon after he recovered he was working on an old building when a stone fell in his eye and he was partially blinded for a few more weeks. There were two odd things about M. Noir. The first was that when he did work, he could do more in one afternoon than anyone we had ever known, more even than the universally competent Marcel. The other was that, though he cursed and swore like the old trooper he was over the slightest thing that went wrong when he was working, he could drop all that and become utterly calm and patient for hours while he fished. He told us that he had sixteen zander in his deep freeze, and backed up his claim by presenting us with two rock-solid fish. Once thawed out and prepared by Marie-Anne with tarragon sauce and new potatoes, they made a superb meal, and an excellent defence against Dr Samuel Johnson's opinion of angling, which was 'A worm at one end of the line and a fool at the other.'

Not many men who go shooting are also anglers, and very few keen fishermen ever go shooting. The difference in appeal between the two activities is underlined by the fact that though there are few women hunters, it is by no means uncommon here to see a woman fishing, fully equipped with the latest gear, and with or without a man in attendance. Anglers are by nature contemplative, whereas hunters rarely think twice about anything. While hunters not infrequently shoot each other in the heat of the moment, it is extremely rare for one angler to hook and land another. I will not say that it has never happened, because for all I know somewhere in a dark corner of the *Guinness Book of Records*, or the *Book of Heroic Failures*, such an event is described. I was once taken trout fishing on the shores of a Swedish lake but caught nothing, though I did manage to hook myself in the lower lip. I might well have done the same to my neighbour. The hook was expertly removed and I was easily persuaded to abandon my efforts while the rest of the group caught numbers of trout which were slowly cooked at the lakeside beach over iron containers full of glowing sawdust. They were delicious, but I have never been fishing since.

I do sometimes idle down the river in a rowing boat, for preference early on a summer morning, or in the late afternoon, as the sun begins to sink. Whatever the time, there are always, during the season, anglers here and there on both wooded banks, enthroned on their platforms, and surveying their little kingdoms in total peace and contentment. When I look down the lovely broad stretch of the river to the distant hills, and see these men, at least for the moment free of care in their leafy surroundings, I do sometimes feel a twinge of envy, and wonder whether I might not buy a fishing rod and become one of them. But I never do; instinct tells me that I would be no good at it.

M. Rambaud was not an angler and, as might be expected, his idea of what to do with a river bank was somewhat unusual. When we first explored the property prior to buying, we found, at a place where the bank made a shelf about fifteen feet wide and about the same height above the water, and was backed by a miniature cliff, an open concrete water tank. Water which dripped down through the rock face filled the tank, about eight feet long by four feet wide and three feet deep, and there was an overflow to regulate the level of water.

This, M. Rambaud told us, was his frog pond, where he had raised edible frogs. It seemed rather small to produce a quantity for the open market, so I presumed he had intended them for his own consumption. Unfortunately, he said, the frogs were not happy there. Some escaped and the others sulked and did not reproduce. He had dropped the idea, and with it his interest in the river bank.

Mme Rambaud also appreciated, briefly, the charms of the water's edge, though not for painting. She did not mind copying the masters, but for her own work she rather looked down on landscape and figurative painting. 'It's so unambitious,' she said. Her use of the river bank, though, as far as I know, an isolated instance, was as unexpected as her husband's. Not long after Jean-Claude, the accountant, had moved into his house, he received an invitation to a 'riverside evening' from Mme Rambaud. It was on the night of St Jean, the French Midsummer's Eve, one of the most important celebrations of the year in southern France, and a favourite night for dances and parties.

Expecting at least cocktails and canapés, Jean-Claude and his lively young wife, Martine, walked the short distance across the fields to the Rambauds' river bank, only to find themselves part of a gathering of local art lovers and literati propped against the trees and strewn among the grass, without a gin and tonic or a peanut in sight. Instead of cocktails, canapés and conversation, Mme Rambaud offered them a long recitation of traditional Midsummer's Eve poetry from medieval times to the present day. It took them well into the twilight of the longest day, and when it was over Mme Rambaud made her offer of a swim in the pool at one franc a time plus a contribution to the expense of the chemicals.

According to the local farmers, anglers are not as harmless as their peace and gentleness suggests. In addition to the river itself, there were a number of small lakes in the area. They dated from the heyday of the railways, between the wars, when a small branch line was constructed to link outlying villages to the main towns. The railway company dug out gravel to form a level bed for the track; the pits filled with water and, over the years, became rich with fish, especially carp, goldfish and tench. All sorts of people from Arab schoolboys to the local curate fished in these lakes. My garden pond is full of goldfish obtained from small boys at one franc a time.

Some of the lakes were bordered by M. Lambert's fields and M. Caumont's orchards. M. Lambert became fed up with people beating a path through his crops to reach his lake, and M. Caumont found trees near his stripped of fruit, and lengths of hose and watering equipment disappeared regularly. They applied to the local council to have their lakes turned into 'décharges'. These are official rubbish dumps where anything except normal household rubbish, by which they mean food and packaging waste, can be thrown away. Gradually the lakes filled up with old mattresses, broken sofas, three-legged chairs, rusty drain pipes, broken asbestos panels, piles of old newspapers and magazines, old gasstoves and refrigerators, any old iron, piles of garden waste from town dwellers who dared not burn it, old clothes, broken tools – anything at all no longer wanted.

One of these dumps was within a kilometre of our house. One day I asked Marcel to get rid of a load of old rubbish which had gradually accumulated in the barn as our restorations were carried out, including M. Rambaud's ancient gas cooker and lawn-mower. We loaded up his lorry and I expected him back within the hour, when he would have unloaded at the dump. He was back within ten minutes.

'You were quick,' I said.

'I had not stopped rolling before Ali Poubelle and his gang were in the back heaving things out,' he said. 'Hardly anything went into the dump. If they are there every day, it's going to take a long time to fill it up.'

In fact it took nearly two years to fill the two lakes, and involved us in several ways. Among the things which people dumped were a great many old tyres, well known for their burning qualities. At one time there was a fire almost every other week. As soon as there were enough tyres for a good blaze, someone set them off, lighting up the sky for miles around. Marie-Anne and I got tired of calling the fire brigade, and they got tired of coming. At first, the chief officer seemed to think it was good practice for the men to turn out, but they soon got round to asking us if it was the same dump, and thanking us for letting them know.

With their usual liberal interpretation of regulations the local people took a wide view of what could be dumped, and they certainly did not exclude household pets. The dumps soon attracted a horde of abandoned and stray dogs and cats. On the colder winter nights some of these strays discovered cosy corners in our barn. One cat had a litter of kittens in the wood pile, and it was not uncommon for me to rouse a mangy dog from its slumbers when I first went into the barn in the mornings.

Once the lakes had been filled and the rubbish dump levelled and covered with new soil, the succession of stray animals came to an end. It was some months later, after the farmers had sown their first crops on the reclaimed land, that one morning I discovered a very small and solitary kitten sitting sadly in the middle of the drive. She was a beautiful little thing with very long hair in wide black and golden stripes, green eyes, and the sort of face that advertises cat food. We really didn't want another cat, but she was irresistible.

We were sure that Cleo would be jealous, and she was. She never seriously attacked Kitty but she repeatedly expressed her strong disapproval by spitting and chasing, and eating Kitty's food whenever she got the chance. Kitty put up with it all with unshakeable calm and good nature and was clearly ready to be friends, but two years of association have not softened Cleo's attitude much, though there are occasional harmonies. On cold nights the need for warmth overcomes antipathy and they lie within a few feet of each other on either side of the fireplace, just keeping a weather eye open. And on sunny days they sit on opposite sides of the goldfish pond, waiting to grab any unwary fish that strays too close to the edge. Two more anglers. I don't mind because their presence keeps away the cheeky kingfisher, a much better angler than they are, which occasionally perches on the head of the stone nymph in the centre of the pool.

Chapter Seventeen

LET'S HAVE A PARTY

There are two ways to live in a country that is not your own. You can take an interest in what goes on around you, the people, their customs, even their history, or you can ignore all that and create your own private 'island'. In France the 'liberté' in the French national motto still means something and, once you have conformed to the regulations, no one will bother you. Personally, I have always been interested in other people's business, so Marie-Anne and I chose the first course, trying to understand the different ways of life, the different behaviour and customs, of our new neighbours. But even as we learned things changed around us.

This was farming country – fruit, vegetables, cereals, wine and livestock. It has been so from time immemorial, and so it still is, but not in the same way. The rhythm and permanence, and the security, have gone from farming. In the past the farmers always had enough. They gave their labour, their expenses were limited, and as a rule they made a profit; some good farmers died rich. But in recent years the consumer society, inflation, increased mechanisation and the establishment of EEC quotas for various products have changed all that.

In this area the shock has been brutal. Only five or six years ago the farmers here had a good investment – the price of agricultural land had been rising every year. There was a shortage of farms to rent, and would-be tenants had to pay a heavy premium similar to 'key money' to get one. Anyone from abroad seeking to buy a landed property risked seeing most of the land taken from them on compulsory purchase by the Sogaf, an official body which would then install new young farmers on it. This organisation no longer has money to spare. The value of the land is in steady decline and the farmers have additional problems.

In some other agricultural parts of France there has been a steady decline for years. In departments like the Hautes-Alpes of Provence, where life has always been hard, it is now almost impossible. Dozens of villages have died. Where there were hundreds of people there are now a few dozen ancients with nothing but bent backs and wrinkled and toothless faces to show for a life of incessant toil. Even in the fertile heart of France, in departments like the Cher, it's the same story: deserted villages, no shops, boarded-up houses, closed schools. Where there were seventy farmers, there are a dozen left, scraping a living.

There are as yet no dead villages in Gascony, but many are struggling, and the farmers are afraid. Much of the land in the river valleys is very fertile, but it is heavy. Traditionally it was ploughed with the aid of horses, sometimes oxen. As long as they worked, the beasts manured the ground, and when they were too old for work, the farmers sold them to the butcher for almost as much as they had paid for them in the first place. Now the farmer must have all the latest agricultural machinery. New tractors cost thousands, old tractors fetch almost nothing. But farming is said to be more efficient, more productive.

M. Caumont questions it all. 'What I know is that I grew up in a happy family. True, we had fewer possessions. We knew less about farming than we know now. I am, perhaps, a better farmer than my father, advances have been made. But my father never owed money, while I float on a sea of debt, like every other farmer I know. Young people, sensibly, don't want to work on the land. Clever men invent machines to do their work, and the farmers must buy them, because they cannot get labour. Where do they get the money? They are obliged to borrow, and in a few years the machines must be replaced, and they borrow again. There is no way out.'

M. Caumont has retired now – a good man, who has worked hard and been respected all his life, long time president of a fruit growers' co-operative. His son has taken over, and has new ideas. M. Caumont watches in resignation tinged with bitterness, as the valley orchards, which he helped his father plant, are torn out to make room for cereal fields. In recent years the lower lying orchards have been affected by frost, while those on the southern slopes of the hills have done better. It needs only one night of late frost to ruin a fruit harvest. This year, after the fruit had set, M. Caumont forecast the largest ever crop from our plum trees, about thirty tons. A late frost in mid-April, the only one of the winter, brought the ultimate harvest down to little more than three tons. M. Caumont, who has apples and pears as well as plums, and whose orchards are ten times as big as ours, reckoned that one frost had cost him forty thousand pounds. So desperate measures were needed on the Caumont farm.

On the other side of us it is a different story. Following her husband's death, Mme Lambert has rented her land to another farmer, M. Martinet, a man of apparently limitless enterprise and energy. Where other farmers can't cope, his answer to the farming crisis is to take some or all of their land, and tackle it like a military campaign. On the fields next to us, which M. Lambert had rented out for a small fortune to a sand and gravel company years before, the topsoil had consequently been removed. When eventually he got the land back, M. Lambert struggled to raise a poor and patchy crop of maize every year. I wanted to buy these fields, about two hectares, and asked M. Caumont's advice. It's poor land, he told me, worth about half the normal rate, not more than four thousand pounds. Mme Lambert, generous as she is in small things, like aubergines and tomatoes, refused to listen to anything less than ten thousand pounds. The fields are still hers, but rented by M. Martinet, who, on the 'poor' land, by dint of incessant watering, succeeded in raising two crops of haricots verts in one summer. It was typical of his approach that within two days of the harvesting of the first crop, the land had been reploughed and resown for a second crop.

So, while some farms get bigger, many are for sale, and, as the farmers are now paid not to produce certain crops, fields are left fallow, and are returning to grass and weeds on all sides. Despite their initial scorn tourism has become an alternative source of income for many farmers, who offer bed and breakfast, or convert old farm buildings to holiday cottages. Down here they don't make the transition from turnips to tourism easily. In Normandy

I once stayed with a successful farmer who had turned part of his land into a well-equipped camp site and was proud of it. He looked indulgently at his campers and said to me, 'Far and away the best crop I ever had.' In contrast a local farmer here asked me if I could help him get holiday visitors for a cottage on his land. I went to look at it. The walls were patterned with damp stains, there was no bathroom, the sideboard had lost part of a leg and was propped up with ancient books a lot more valuable than the furniture, and, if it had been London, I would have said the mattresses came from a skip. When I told him he would have to redecorate and refurnish throughout and put in a bathroom, his face fell.

'But that would cost money,' he said. He was typical of many peasant farmers. They have learned that if they want a good crop, they must invest in fertiliser, but they want a return from tourism without any investment.

One of the lovely sights of spring when we first came here, was the great drifts of rose and pink blossom as the many peach orchards came into flower. But the farmers decided that they could no longer compete with Spanish growers who could get their peaches to market about two weeks before the first local peaches were ready. So many of the peach orchards have gone.

There is change everywhere. Even our peaceful river now boasts a beautifully converted barge on which holiday visitors, old people's clubs and others enjoy a daily cruise in summer. In a comfortable dining saloon meals are supplied by one of the best local restaurants, and the strains of music float across the water, where before there was only the plop of a fish or the harsh squawk of the buzzard.

All these are physical changes and have altered the nature and the look of the countryside around us to some extent. But the difference is minor. Those visitors who have not seen it before find a lovely landscape of gently rolling hills, broad valleys with great rivers, smaller valleys with streams and lakes, and wooded slopes as well as farm fields and orchards.

Yes, the land is beautiful, and benevolent, and spacious. But there is more to living in a foreign country than scenery and sunshine, and more than can be learned even in many holidays and

business visits. There is another climate, that created by the people
and their attitudes of mind. It would be a rash man who said he
understands the French. Even after years of living among them
they remain enigmatic, difficult to know in depth.

In general, certain characteristics are strongly marked. 'The
Gallic temperament is impetuous, unreliable, ingenious, inconsist-
ent . . . brave but utterly devoid of that stern temper that survives
defeat . . . They are politically instable, and their plans follow an
ever-varying pattern of emotionalism . . . They stop every travel-
ler, willing or not, and ask him what he knows on any topic that
interests them . . . They are credulous, and slaves of superstition.'
These comments and many others were made by Julius Caesar,
one of the shrewdest and most capable men in history, more than
two thousand years ago, and recorded in his own account of the
conquest of Gaul, *De Bello Gallico*.

Nothing much has changed through the centuries. Their politics
are still chaotic; in sport they do well when winning but lose heart
as soon as they sense defeat. They still repeatedly question
everybody on everything – the public opinion poll is an obsession
in France, and no politician is interviewed without being faced
with the week's result on this or that. Judging by the large number
of advertisements for fortune tellers, clairvoyants and faith healers
they are still credulous. In money matters they are avaricious, but
their insistence on value for money has a good side. The general
high standard of workmanship throughout France is a direct
result. In business they seek an advantage relentlessly and are
dissatisfied when their terms are met, thinking they might have
done better.

They live in this beautiful land, but they are not happy. Their
lives are clouded by mistrust. They have little confidence in each
other. Unlike Britain, where – another generalisation – people
tend to be trusted until they show a good reason why they should
not be, in France all relationships begin in mistrust and suspicion.
Even marriage includes a written contract relating to the material
possessions of the couple. The French countryman cannot take
things at face value, he always suspects an underlying motive.

When you live among them, you cannot help feeling that deep
down the French are a sad race. 'Gay Paree' is a misnomer with a

touch of desperation about it. It was no accident that Françoise Sagan's *Bonjour Tristesse* was a bestseller. Its title, a 'cri de coeur' they all recognised, would have sold it to the French, whoever had written it. In *Madame Bovary* Gustave Flaubert dispassionately describes another aspect of this same sickness. The French soul is often like a caged animal, hopelessly moving around in search of a way out. All their best songs, and there are many lovely ones, are full of nostalgia, of 'tristesse', the sense of something lost from life. One of France's finest and most popular singers, Francis Cabrel, is a Gascon whose songs are poetic in their sadness.

But there are many contradictions in the Gascon character. For me there is a touch of the Irish about them, always ready to be dramatic and voluble, and sometimes rash. I once worked for a time in a small town in the far west of Ireland, in county Mayo. The local hero was a young man who had inherited a country house and a fortune in his twenties. He was not envied or respected for that, but because in less than ten years he had gone through the lot, spent it all, in the correct Irish order, on horses, drink and women. No true Gascon could bring himself to do that, they have too much respect for money, but like the men of Mayo, they would all like to, and would have admired him for it. Even sober M. Caumont saw the point, when I told him this story before he made a trip to Ireland. 'Ten years of good living is more than most of us ever get,' he said.

The Gascons are fiercely independent, fiery and impetuous, and brave, and if these qualities sometimes degenerate into touchiness and a swaggering boastfulness with a somewhat cavalier regard for truth, it is never long before their joviality and natural courtesy return.

They do appreciate a good lie, and every year in the village of Moncrabeau a Liars' Festival is held and whoever, in the opinion of the judges, tells the most entertaining lie is crowned King (or on one occasion Queen) of the Liars for a year. It has become a popular event which now attracts competitors from all over France, but the point is that it was originally a local, purely Gascon festival.

The exaggeration, the boastfulness, the conscious geniality so often found in the Gascons is, perhaps, just the other side of the coin, a kind of defiance of underlying unhappiness. Perhaps their inability to keep a promise, proverbial in France, is another aspect of the same feeling, as if they ask themselves – what does it matter in the end? Yet they are not men of straw. They are traditionally great fighters. The Three Musketeers were Gascons. The famous d'Artagnan was from a poor farm – it still exists – in the heart of Gascony, though in real life he was a career soldier with no more flair or imagination than the average sergeant-major. He was one of the many younger sons of poor landowners whose only choice in the seventeenth and eighteenth centuries was between poverty on the land and a career with the sword, and who, as the 'cadets de Gascogne', won a reputation for bravery in the king's army. The courage of the Gascons was again evident in World War II when the region was a stronghold of the Resistance.

Another contradiction is that, though tight with money, like all the French, they can be hospitable to strangers. An aged relative of mine went for a walk on a summer's day, forgot where he was, and found himself adrift in a local farmyard. The farmer welcomed him, offered him a draught of some home-made nectar, and after an amiable but incoherent conversation – neither spoke the other's language – steered him in the right direction. He returned to the house even unsteadier on his feet than usual, and saying what remarkably good stuff it was they drink in these parts.

Although the Gascon is often intense and serious, and seldom light-hearted, he can show a spontaneous warmth. The local people, whatever their problems and however cautious they may be in friendship, are also unfailing in their courtesy in day to day matters. They would not dream of passing you or anyone they know without a friendly 'Bonjour' and the inevitable handshake.

So life goes on, for the most part pleasantly and efficiently enough, though there is a continual round of strikes and demonstrations by the unhappy farmers. They pelt the Town Hall, and the mayor, who has a food canning factory, with the tomatoes he hasn't bought from them, or tip tons of apples into the streets, or block the bridges across the Garonne with their tractors, as they have done once or twice. As the bridges are as much as twenty miles apart, this is a serious inconvenience to those who want to cross and go about their business, but down here the sympathy is

The village of Cassenevil.

with the farmers, and after a short grumble, the motorists wait patiently. They know quite well that no farmer is going to miss his lunch for a demonstration and that shortly before twelve the tractors will start to move.

The French as a whole and the Gascons in particular seem to have two favourite antidotes to their dissatisfactions, sport and television. The regional newspaper *Sud Ouest* devotes from a fifth to a quarter of its pages to sport, plus a ten-page supplement on Mondays. Rugby football is the first great enthusiasm, but almost all popular sports are played and reported at length. The exception is cricket. I have never been a cricket fan, in the real English sense, but when we lived in Westminster we used to like to drive out occasionally in summer to Putney or Richmond and sit under the trees to watch weekend cricket on the green. It's something we miss. Even Marie-Anne, who has no more idea of the game than I have of dress design, enjoyed this. She thought the men in their white flannels looked very chic against the green grass and trees.

Instead of cricket on the green, we have 'pétanque', a form of bowls, in the village squares. The word 'petanque' is a dialect contraction of 'pieds tanques', which means 'with feet fixed', because the players must play standing still or crouched with their feet inside a small circle. In a similar game, 'boules Lyonnaises', they are allowed a few steps in launching the bowls. Pétanque is a crafty and contentious game, dear to the unemployed and retired, but as a spectator sport it is hardly in the same category as cricket. Old pullovers, shapeless trousers and carpet slippers do not have the same eye appeal as white flannels, nor bare earth as greensward. Nor do the actions of the players, sometimes varied it is true by players who pick up the metallic bowls with a magnet on a string, to save bending arthritic knees, compare in dramatic interest with the fast bowler's thundering run-up, the wicket keeper's return, the batsmen's different strokes, intended or accidental, the occasional shattering of the wicket, and the grave, processional march to and from the pavilion. It is a game in which some ingenious forms of cheating are practised. The bowls are metal, but hollow, and there are players who drill small holes and pour a little mercury into the interior. This has the effect of shortening the distance the ball will roll once it hits the ground. In competition games it is quite usual for the referee to call for a sudden check on all the bowls in use, and this is done in a kind of cradle where the bowl is rolled from side to side. The 'wrong 'uns' don't roll far enough up the opposite slope. Another tactic, harder to detect, consists in making temporary changes in the playing surface. This is often rough and uneven, with some loose earth or sand, and even small bits of gravel lying on top. The wide, flat carpet slippers have other advantages apart from comfort; a slight movement of the foot can dislodge a significant amount of sand in the right direction. Was it absent-minded, accidental, intended?

As for television, the hard-working farmers and artisans take it as a substitute for sleeping pills. French television is hypnotic in its monotony and awfulness. It seems to be trapped in a time warp. Programmes which were running when we arrived here ten years ago are still running, on the same nights of the week, at the same hour, with the same presenters, with the same empty smiles, and the same singers. They have not returned, they have never been away. 'Stars' who should have been allowed to retire gracefully years ago are still dragged regularly before the cameras. It would not surprise me to see one pushed up to the microphone in a wheelchair. Even when they die, television won't leave them in peace. People like Coluche, a famous comedian, and Thierry Le Luron, an impressionist, both dead for several years, still appear regularly every few weeks in television programmes.

No original plays are written for French television; instead there are endless quiz programmes with consumer goods as prizes. Apart from imported American soaps and a few French detectives, Maigret and imitators, there are no series, nothing like *Minder* or *Rumpole of the Bailey* or *The Darling Buds of May*. There are few discussions, no orchestral music. On top of its inadequacy as entertainment, French television is abused by the government and its politicians, from the President downwards, who use it incessantly to tell the people how great France is, how they are leading this field and that. One is driven to suppose that this constant need to say how marvellous they are must cloak a serious inferiority complex. But the average Gascon has no respect whatever for the politicians of Paris. The wide streak of corruption in French society which has become visible in recent years does nothing to help the political image. One scandal succeeds another, involving politicians from government ministers to mayors of provincial towns, all with their hand in the till for millions of francs. Several presidents of football clubs have joined in the fun, as well as heads of big business. President Mitterrand has had nothing to say on the subject. No wonder the average Gascon looks on all the flattery and ego boosting as a cheap attempt to get votes. We used to grumble about British television but we would swap it very willingly for the French product. It is a disgrace to a nation that calls itself intelligent.

Outside the house the French like big parties. Every Gascon village has its annual fete day, when they hang out the flags, dust down the village band, set up stalls and side-shows and compete for prizes. From time to time they have other social evenings associated with card games, boules, rugby or other sports. The prizes at these affairs are invariably edible, eventually, though often still alive when handed over – fat pigs, turkeys, geese or even rabbits.

The biggest party of all is on the National Day, 14th July. This holiday is celebrated with a great deal of verve everywhere. In our local town restaurants which have no terrace are allowed to put tables out under the trees in the various squares, the trees are decorated with coloured lights, and in the main square a stage is set up and an orchestra plays, and an area is roped off for dancing.

But the great event of the day is the late evening firework display. Not the least astonishing thing about it is its splendour. The question which is invariably asked in almost all other circumstances, 'Who is going to pay?', is apparently ignored on this occasion. The Gascons take an almost childish delight in fireworks, and our English visitors are always surprised at the scope and lavishness of this display. It takes place near one of the bridges, from barges moored in the centre of the river, and from part of the south bank. It seems that the whole town as well as people from miles around come in their thousands to watch. The bridge and both river banks are packed with spectators, and every vantage point is occupied.

The show begins at 10 p.m. with rockets that go off with a series of bangs which reverberate like heavy artillery and frighten the small children, but not too much. There follows an hour-long exhibition of whizzers and bangers and hummers and rockets full of coloured starbursts and every ingenious device known to firework makers. Each new splendour is greeted by gasps of admiration from the massed crowds, and the final arc of coruscating stars and the enormous bang which closes the show raise a spontaneous cheer of appreciation. The crowd makes its way back to the leafy squares, some homeward bound, some to dine, some to dance. In these hard times there is a touch of 'bread and circuses' about it, but it's none the worse for that. It makes a great night out. When a French friend asked what was our national day, I had to think before saying, 'I suppose it's St George's Day, at least in England,' and when he followed up with 'How do you celebrate it?', I could only say, 'We don't.'

These are the people we deal with every day, a mercurial race, full of awareness, who feel that life could and should offer a lot more than it does, and in consequence they feel cheated and often tend to react bitterly. Discontent is a very strong flavour in the French brew, and the Gascons are no exception.

Yet, and it is part of the enigma, as we have discovered, when they let themselves go, they really know how to enjoy themselves. One occasion we shall always remember was the 'méchoui' arranged by my friend, the lady of the bath, at the local auberge. 'Méchoui' is a term originally used throughout the Maghreb – Arab North Africa – for barbecueing a whole sheep. What Madame was offering was an alfresco dinner based on such a barbecue. For eighty francs we would have aperitifs, soup, barbecued lamb, pudding and free wine, followed by music and dancing. And that's what we had, plus some unexpected extras.

We had an English family on holiday in the pigeonnier. Dad was a highly placed aviation executive, Mum taught handicapped children and there were two small boys, six and nine years old, John and Peter. Marie-Anne and I thought they might find the méchoui interesting. An old friend of ours, a writer and artist, was actually staying in the inn, with his wife and son, so we bought our tickets and formed a small British delegation to this essentially French affair.

Having had a drink at the house, we arrived a few minutes later than the seven thirty advertised. The inn has a spacious courtyard, shaded by large chestnut trees. Long trestle tables had been set out in rows beneath the trees with places for about seventy people. In the courtyard between the parking area and the tables there was a pit with a whole sheep stretched on a spit above a miserable fire. Edward, the artist, and family, being resident, were already there, installed at a table facing the abandoned sheep, drinks at hand. Apart from a French family of five at the far end of a table, the place appeared deserted.

'Bit of a rave up,' said our aviation friend laconically.

'Madame says not to worry,' said Edward. 'Plenty of people coming. Full house. Just southern time-keeping.'

Madame of the bath spotted us and brought us a kir all round, and Coke for the boys. We chatted. Nothing happened for a while, then other guests began to arrive. On her way back from serving them we stopped Madame and asked her when things would get going.

'We can't start yet,' she said. 'The cooks are not here.' Then she added, by way of explanation, 'They are the local dustmen and they haven't finished their round yet.'

'Did she say the cooks are the dustmen?' asked Edward's wife, tentatively.

'That's right.'

'Just as well we are not having stew,' said the aviation man.

Madame, who speaks no English, saw us smile, and smiled herself. 'Don't worry. They will soon be here. Have another kir.'

Five minutes later the three Moroccan cooks, still in their boots and jerkins, appeared, and were greeted with a ragged cheer. One of them began kicking up the fire, and added more logs. A second produced a galvanised bucket full of oil.

'I saw him fetch that oil from the garage next door,' said Edward, improvising, as the third man produced a floor mop, dipped it in the bucket and began to slosh oil all over the sheep.

'I bet his wife's looking for that mop,' said the aviation man, not to be outdone.

By now the tables were practically full, and a cloud of pungent blue smoke was drifting under the trees. Conversation all round was becoming animated, but there was no sign of the meal starting. Madame appeared again, as if in answer to a telepathic command.

'Won't be long now,' she said. 'Have another kir.'

'I think I'd prefer a gin and tonic,' said Edward. 'All right, all round?' No one protested. 'Okay. Six gin and tonics, madame, if you please.'

They had barely arrived when the meal began. Madame's son went round putting open bottles of red wine on the table, one for every four guests. He was followed by his blonde wife, ladling out soup from a huge tureen. After the soup, there was what the French call a 'petit pause', which can last anything up to half an hour. The pause was naturally filled with glasses of red wine, conversation and repetitions of the bucket of oil and mop routine. As we talked, we discovered that the lively lady opposite me and most of our immediate neighbours were from Calais.

'You are Eengleesh,' said the man sitting next to her. 'When ze Eengleesh arrive in Calais, we lock up our women,' he added, glancing at his companion. From her subsequent behaviour, it might have been an idea to lock her up whoever arrived in Calais.

Time went by, and we were beginning to lose interest in whether we had anything more to eat or not, but spirits were raised when the sheep was removed from the spit and placed on a butcher's table, where one of the cooks attacked it ferociously with a scimitar, or something very like it. While this was going on, to shouts of encouragement from the diners, and stares of incredulity from the two small boys, huge dishes of rice appeared and were placed at intervals along the tables. Gradually plates bearing roast lamb were passed down the table. Edward and the aviation man received beautifully cooked slices of leg, while Marie-Anne and I each had an interesting collection of bones with a few tatters of meat adhering. They came round again with more bottles of wine. And again. It was quite good, if you drank enough of it.

Some time after the main course, the moment for which the small boys had been patiently waiting all evening arrived – ice-cream was passed round, with double portions for them as the only small children present. While this was going on Madame's son and daughter went round the tables with a seemingly endless piece of string, linking all the diners together. The women were apparently told to loop it around a bra strap or through their blouse, and the men to attach it to their trousers. I had no idea what was going on but it was obvious that most of the diners had played this game before and knew what to expect. Marie-Anne had quickly appreciated how things were going to turn out and only pretended to attach it, and advised Edward's wife and Mrs Aviation to do the same.

Eventually amid a good deal of hilarity the string was pulled, and when the confusion which followed had subsided, a number of the women, who had not been wearing much anyway on the hot summer evening, were in advanced stages of undress, and several of the men had lost their shorts or trousers. The lively lady across the table was topless and stood up waving her shirt.

'Oh, not again, Mum,' said a pretty teenage girl a couple of places away to my left. Whether she meant that Mum did this every year, or every week, or wherever she could find a méchoui, we never knew. But Mum, who was directly opposite me, was bouncing around unrestrained, and for a woman with a teenage daughter she was remarkably well built and had nothing to be ashamed of. To keep up the liveliness, the man next to her, reduced to his colourful underpants, stood on the bench and sang, quite well, what Marie-Anne said was a distinctly lewd song. Nevertheless, almost everybody present, men and women, knew the chorus and joined in heartily.

Satisfied with his triumph, he sat down and said, 'Now you give us Eengleesh song.'

I demurred, thinking that we would make a very poor choral group, but Marie-Anne, among whose many qualities is the ability to smooth over awkward moments, broke into 'Happy birthday to you', and in no time everybody joined in, and honour was saved. After this, there was a pause for breath and drinks, and a what now? feeling. Away to our left an oldish man, grey-haired, ordinary looking, stood up. There was a drop in conversation as people looked in his direction, and I heard a small voice say, 'Mais non, Pappy.' But Grandpa took no notice. He remained standing and began to sing.

Whatever we expected, it was not what we got. The songs he sang were well-known, sentimental, musical comedy hits of the recent past, and he sang them in a full tenor voice without the slightest false note or hesitation. Each was greeted enthusiastically with a round of energetic applause. The word was passed around the tables, 'He's retired now, but for twenty years he was a soloist with the Opéra Comique in Paris.' During the third song he encouraged the diners to join in, and not for the first time I was surprised at the musicality and choral ability of the French. The old man bowed slightly and sat down, happy, like all performers with an appreciative audience. He had added a touch of champagne to an already warm-hearted evening.

Madame came round to announce that the occasion would continue with music and dancing. People began to leave the tables and move to the bar. Mum was persuaded to put her shirt on to go indoors. 'Good night, les Anglais,' called her retrousered friend, entering the bar.

We took the small boys home, tired out, mystified by the unfamiliar goings-on, but well content with their ice-cream. Edward and family stayed behind, and reported later that the revelry continued until well after midnight.

Next time I saw Madame, I complimented her on the evening and said how much everyone had enjoyed themselves.

'It's the same every year,' she said. 'It's the sunshine and the air of Gascony. It goes to their heads.'

Gascony is one of the last unspoiled regions of France. One of the things we like most of all is the feeling of space, that towns and villages are miles apart and not linked by ribbon development, the sense that there is room to live, and for people and places to evolve in their own way. I don't think the French could live happily in a small country, crowded together. The Dutch would manage very well in France, but the French in a space like Holland would be a total disaster. As it is the open spaces, the distances, are their consolation, their margin of liberty. They walk, they climb, they sail, and in the space and the open air something of that 'tristesse' disperses.

We share this sense of liberty, and we like, too, a lifestyle where a village may have three bakers each baking their own 'real' bread, and where farmers still have their own vineyard and make their own wine, and where there are markets in every town which have been taking place on the same days every week for a thousand years, and are still crammed with the produce of the local fields and woods and orchards.

And their land, their beloved Gascony, with its rolling hills, its forests and woods, its fertile fields, its countless streams and lakes, and its great rivers, all sheltered by the majestic barrier of the snow-capped Pyrenees, is itself a daily benediction.

Recently we were away for six weeks in London, the longest period we have ever been absent. It seemed to us that life was becoming increasingly stressful in London, and we were pleased to return to Gascony.

The baker calls three times a week. He is the epitome of peasant reserve and caution, always a formal 'bonjour', but rarely volunteering a comment of any kind, and in the years I have known him, I don't think he has ever handed me a loaf without first having the money for it in his hand. Then he gives me the change, if any is due, and then he gives me the loaf. When I returned, he started deliveries again. On the first day he said, 'Bonjour, monsieur,' and held his hand out of the window of his van for me to shake, something he had never done before. 'Did you have a good trip?'

'Very good,' I said. 'We have a grandson, our first. Everything's fine. My wife is staying on another week to help my daughter-in-law.'

'That's good. All that's very good. I'll come by on Saturday as usual. It's nice to see you back.'

Well, I thought, as I walked back into the house with the country loaf in my hand, perhaps I do belong here at last. On the other hand it might be just that I represent three loaves a week all year round, with extras for family and friends in the summer.

You never know with the Gascons. We don't mind. We took a leap in the dark, but looking back on our years here, it seems to us that, on the whole, like the man who fell off the precipice, we've been lucky.